This series will provide guide for all students to th complex and varied landfo Isles.

In this volume P area from t' Scottish ment

The geomorphology
of the British Isles

General editors:
Eric H Brown and Keith Clayton

Northern England

In the same series

Scotland   *J B Sissons*

In preparation

Wales and Southwest England
Eric H Brown, D Q Bowen & R S Waters

Southeast and Southern England   *D K C Jones*

Midlands and Eastern England
Keith Clayton & Allan Straw

Ireland   *G L Davies & N Stephens*

Northern England

Cuchlaine A M King

Methuen & Co Ltd

First published in 1976 by
Methuen & Co. Ltd, 11 New Fetter Lane, London EC4P 4EE

Printed in Great Britain by Butler & Tanner Ltd. Frome & London

ISBN 0 416 84450 2 (hardback edition)
ISBN 0 416 84460 X (paperback edition)

Distributed in the USA by
Harper & Row Publishers Inc. Barnes & Noble Import Division

Contents

Continued

General Editors' Preface

The British Isles is a most varied and complex part of the world, and over a long period it has been studied in great detail by geologists and geomorphologists. Several general studies of the geology and scenery type have appeared, but despite the wealth of the published literature, more detailed work has been limited to a few regions. Indeed although the most ambitious work, Wooldridge and Linton on Southeast England was first published in 1938, no comparable volume has covered any other part of England.

The main difficulty facing anyone writing about the land forms of the British Isles and their history is the paradox that despite a very considerable literature, the gaps and uncertainties seem to diminish very little over the years. It is often said that each piece of research exposes half a dozen new problems, and so far most of the published literature has tended to add to the complexity of our knowledge. The only way out of this problem is through the establishment of more general concepts into which this detail will fit, and this is the role of this series of books on the different parts of the British Isles. The synthesis is certainly not easy, and it is obviously incomplete. Our understanding of the present land surface and its relationship with the underlying geology (whether 'solid' or 'drift') is relatively secure, but the historical background to the present, complicated as it is by the fluctuating environments of Quaternary time, is less well known. Each author has brought his own special interests and expertise to the synthesis of the region he knows best. To conclude the series, a summary volume by the editors will seek common strands in the regional summaries and erect a national framework within which the more detailed regional accounts will fit.

While no standard approach has been imposed on the contributing authors, care has been taken to be consistent in the use of terminology and the recently-elaborated Quaternary time-scale (Mitchell *et al* 1973) has everywhere been used. Correlation tables are provided for each region, while the maps and diagrams will be found particularly valuable since those in the published literature are so scattered, and generally refer to quite small areas. Above all these volumes will make the existing literature accessible to the greater number who seek a wider evolutionary understanding of the landforms of the very diverse regions of the British Isles.

I Structure – landform relationships

The geomorphological character of Northern England is strongly dependent upon the rock type and the structural elements. Almost all the pre-Quaternary rocks belong to the Palaeozoic period. Many different rocks of this period are represented and these play an important part in determining the various landscape elements. The region can be divided into landscape types largely on the basis of rock type and structure, although in some of the lowland areas more recent drift deposits determine the characteristics of the landforms.

In parts of Northern England nearly horizontal rock strata of varied lithology control the landscape, but elsewhere the scenery is developed on relatively homogeneous but strongly contorted rocks. Examples of these two contrasting types of structural control are found in the Yorkshire Dales (Clayton 1966) and the Howgill Fells respectively (Marr and Fearnsides 1909). Evidence of former stages of landscape development can most safely be sought in the latter area, while the former provides valuable examples of the effect of rock type on landscape forms. Karst forms associated with limestone outcrops are particularly significant in this area.

Northern England as covered in this book is mainly an area of uplands, but these vary greatly in character within the area, and are separated by areas of lower elevation. True lowlands are restricted to fairly small areas. The structural relationships in the landscape can best be studied by describing the contrasting elements that make up the landscape. The area can be broadly divided into upland regions on the one hand, and, on the other, their fringing scarps and the relatively small areas of lowlands. The divisions are shown on fig. 1.1. The uplands can be divided

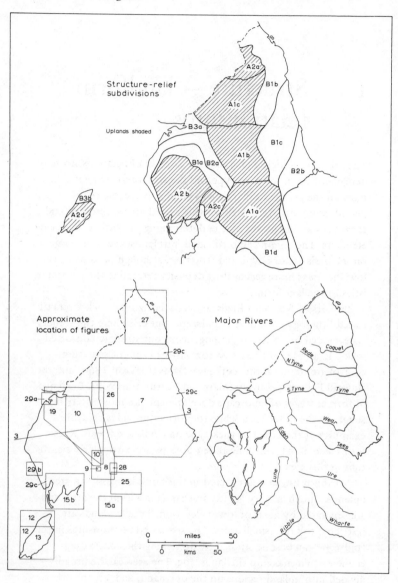

Fig. 1.1. Regional subdivisions and the main drainage lines. The position of figures within the region is shown.

into two main groups. These are the relatively rigid blocks of the Pennines, which determine the major character of the central part of the area. These blocks stretch in a belt from south to north, and in them rocks mostly of Carboniferous age outcrop. The other major group consists of Lower Palaeozoic uplands in parts of which igneous rocks dominate the landscape. The Cheviot Hills and the Lake District Hills form the major elements on the mainland, while the higher, southern part of the Isle of Man continues this type of scenery across the Irish Sea to the west, (see figs. 1.1, 1.2 and 1.3).

Structural elements
One of the major structural features of Northern England is the Great sigma-shaped fault system that separates the Pennine blocks from the Lake District and surrounding lowland areas. These low-

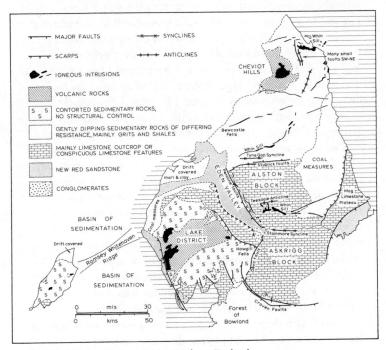

Fig. 1.2 Structural elements in Northern England.

lands include the Tyne valley to the north, the Eden valley in the northwest, and the Craven lowlands to the southwest. These major fault systems, shown in fig. 1.2, include the Stublick faults, the Pennine faults and the Dent and Craven systems.

The Caledonian earth movements had important effects in the Pennines (P.E. Kent 1974), which are broadly anticlinal Carboniferous areas, separating Mesozoic basins. The older Palaeozoic outcrop in Ribblesdale, Ingleton area and upper Teesdale within the Pennine blocks. The Lower Palaeozoic rocks of the Pennines are probably shelf or marginal types, and are thinner than those in the Caledonian geosyncline. In the Caledonian orogeny granite intrusion occurred, and this may have helped to initiate the present Pennine blocks. Geophysical data have revealed the positive anomalies over the Alston and Askrigg blocks, resulting from shallow granites in the basement rocks. These granites may form the northwest part of an arc running through eastern England to join the Ardennes. There was more than one phase of movement in the Caledonian orogeny, as indicated in the Lake District, where Ordovician Borrowdale Volcanic series rest on folded and eroded Skiddaw Slates of Arenig and Llanvirn age. The Silurian of the Pennines strike at a different angle to the underlying Ingletonian, at 110 and 135 degress respectively. Granite cores have been proved in the Alston and Askrigg blocks, and probably also occur in the Derbyshire Dome to the south.

The whole area became consolidated and shield-like as a result of the Caledonian orogeny, and only the shale-filled basins and gulfs of the lower Carboniferous were affected seriously by the Hercynian orogeny. The Caledonian Weardale granite was unroofed in pre-Carboniferous times. indicating that post-Caledonian erosion of the Pennines must have measured thousands of metres due to differential uplift accompanied by sinking of the surrounding basins. This irregular landscape was buried by Carboniferous sediments. Initial coarse clastic sediments indicate the strong relief. The Carboniferous sedimentation was dominated by block and basin control, and mineralised areas are associated with the underlying granites. The blocks show slow interrupted subsidence. Thicker sediments accumulated in the subsiding gulfs and basins around the blocks, the subsidence in

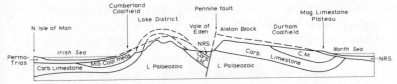

Fig. 1.3 Generalised geological section running west to east across the area. Based on the Geological Survey maps.

them being two to three times that of the blocks. The Millstone Grit deposition was controlled by similar but smaller structural movements. The relative buoyancy of the blocks was dying away in the Coal Measure period.

In the Lake District, where Lower Palaeozoic rocks outcrop over the whole central area, the Borrowdale Volcanic series are very resistant, and have exerted an effect on all later deformation, (Moseley 1973). The volcanoes were related to an island arc system associated with continental drift and sea floor spreading. The Caledonian continental collision was the next important event, creating northeast folds and northwest and north faults. The limestones of the Morecambe Bay area reflect the northsouth structures of the older rocks. There are also northwest and northeast shear structures, resulting from the eastwest stresses of Armorican date. Structural events from the early Palaeozoic to the present day have played a part also, including later tensional modifications.

The main effect of the Armorican and Alpine earth movements in the stable block areas was faulting, when the major Craven, Dent, Pennine and Stublick faults moved, with locally displacements exceeding 2000 m. The Hercynian earth movements did not seriously contort the more rigid parts of the area, and the stresses were mainly tensional, with vertical movements predominating, sometimes reaching thousands of metres, as during the deposition of the Carboniferous strata. Long-continued secular tilting has continued through to the Alpine orogeny and Neogene periods. The basins to the south show strong folding, by contrast. The Dent fault is monoclinal in form, with an east-facing vertical limb, while the other is horizontal. The Hutton monocline is similar. Faults have dominant trends that are northwest, north and northeast. There are also eastwest faults between the Alston and Askrigg blocks. The northerly faults are mainly related to the vertical limbs of monoclinal structures, such as the Dent fault. The northwest faults are much more numerous, and occur most frequently around the stable blocks. The latest phase of movement on the Craven faults has caused a southwesterly downthrow in the Tertiary, resulting from the uplift of the Askrigg block relative to the Irish Sea basin. The northeast faults are generally smaller. Joint trends are parallel to the fault trends, but are distinct in origin. In steeply dipping rocks the joint pattern is related to the fold pattern.

The structural history of the Pennine fault system as described by M.H.P. Bott (1974) can be reconciled with Hercynian structures and with the occurrence of Whin sill or dyke pebbles in the Upper Brockram. Four stages can be identified and are illustrated diagrammatically in fig. 1.4.

(a) Hercynian eastwest compression produced reversed and thrust faults along the Inner Pennine fault line, and a syncline formed in the Vale of Eden, giving a topographic ridge on the western, upthrow side of the fault, and a depression in the Vale of Eden. The Alston block was not depressed, and the Whin sill was intruded into the lower Carboniferous rocks of the Alston block, but it did not extend west of the fault.

(b) Erosion removed the topographic ridge along the fault, and possibly formed an early Pennine scarp, exposing the Whin sill and dykes. The basal Permo-Triassic sediments collected in the Eden valley, and overlapped onto the lower Palaeozoic rocks adjacent to the inner fault.

(c) The Eden valley went on subsiding during the Permo-Triassic sedimentation, controlled by basement faulting parallel to the Pennine fault line and may have been related to eastwest tension associated with the opening of the North Atlantic ocean. Differential subsidence ceased at the end of the Permo- Trias and Mesozoic rocks may have been deposited over the whole area.

(d) Tertiary faulting along the outer Pennine fault line occurred with downthrow to the west, and uplift to the Pennine block. The Cross Fell inlier occurs where this fault lies to the west of the inner Pennine fault. Further north the Tertiary fault

lies to the east of the inner, older fault, as in the diagram, so that
the Permo-Triassic rocks transgress over the lower Palaeozoic.
The outer fault has a throw of about 300 m. The Whin sill

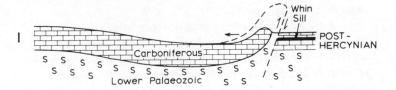

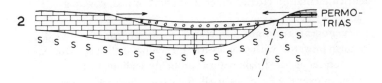

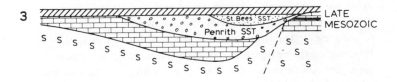

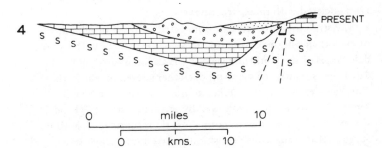

Fig. 1.4 Diagram of possible structural history of the Pennine fault line
and the Vale of Eden in four stages. (After Bott 1974).

pebbles in the Upper Brockram can be explained in this way. The northeast dip of the Carboniferous and the Permo-Trias off the Lake District towards the Pennine faults is thus attributed to the Hercynian and Permo-Triassic earth movements, rather than to those in the Tertiary period.

Folds in the Hercynian movements were gentle in the blocks, for example the Richmond anticline, while in the Craven lowlands folds had greater amplitudes of 300 to 800 m and lengths of up to 15 km. Faulted troughs developed in the Permian and continued to subside through the Trias, with more than 3000 m of New Red sandstone collecting in the Cheshire basin. In Yorkshire a peneplaned surface cut across the Carboniferous trends and sedimentation crossed older strata northwards, covering a flattish surface.

Epeirogenic tectonics characterise Yorkshire from the mid-Permian onwards, with progressive thickening to the east. During the Cretaceous, the Chalk sea was probably shallow, if it extended over the Pennines at all, the Palaeozoic rocks being near sea level. An easterly tilting was the dominant post-Cretaceous movement. As the Chalk subsided below the Tertiary in the North Sea basin, so the Pennine area rose 500 to 700 m. This was probably a long-continued movement from early Eocene to the present. The largest movement was probably during the Pliocene, on the evidence of erosion surfaces, and it was, therefore, post-Alpine in age. The hinge line lies along the high western edge of the Pennines, with basins developed to the west in the Permo-Triassic period. The movement along the boundary faults are associated with these structural events.

The structural processes are connected with the development of cyclothems in the Carboniferous strata, especially in the Yoredale Series of the Yorkshire Dales. W.H.C. Ramsbottom (1973, 1974) has summarised views on cyclothem development in the Yoredale Series. Hudson, Dunham, Bott and Johnson favour repeated tectonic uplift, followed by erosion to base level and the influx of the sea due to normal sea floor subsidence. Moore suggests that arenaceous deposition ceased in each cycle as a result of diversion of the main distributaries. Eustatic rises of sea level of only a few metres would move the coastline and accompanying delta front many kilometres northwards, allowing deposition of limestone. He states 'such an interpretation is supported by the fact that the onset of widespread minor cyclicity begins in many areas of Europe and North America at the same time.' This movement was probably accompanied by continuous subsidence; eustatic controls seem important and the transgression was more rapid than the regression. The cause of the eustatic fluctuations is not known, but was probably not glacial.

The hidden structure of the Lake District and surrounding area is revealed by the geological and structural interpretation of a gravity survey, analysed by M.H.P. Bott (1974). The area is dominated by a west to east belt of low Bouguer anomaly, which reaches minima over exposed granites in Eskdale, Shap and Skiddaw. These probably represent parts of a large batholith under the northern and central Lake District. The granite appears to extend 7 to 10 km deep with outward sloping margins. One shallow ridge connects Eskdale and Shap, and another Ennerdale, St John's, Threlkeld and the Skiddaw granites. The Shap granite is probably connected to the Weardale granite by a deep granite ridge, running between Penrith and Appleby from southwest to northeast, as shown in fig. 1.5.

The present and past uplift of the Lake District is associated with the granite mass deficiency, estimated at 1.1×10^{18} g, and is equal to the present elevation of the Lake District above a 82 m datum. The low gravity values in the Vale of Eden indicate that Permo-Triassic rocks are at least 1 km thick northeast of Penrith. They probably formed during contemporaneous subsidence.

The analysis of the structural elements, in particular the presence of light granites beneath the surface over parts of northern England, provides useful evidence in interpreting the morphology, especially in connection with the development of erosion surfaces.

The Uplands

Pennines

The Forest of Bowland The Forest of Bowland is an upland

region developed on the Namurian rocks of the Upper Carboniferous, which in this area consist mainly of shales and sandstones.
The higher parts of the uplands are free of drift above about
430 m and here the control of the rock type on the landscape
can be seen. On the whole there is a close correspondence
between the structural surfaces and the relief, as pointed out by
Moseley (1961). This is particularly apparent in the northern part
of the area, where many of the slopes follow the dip. Littledale
Fell, rising to over 490 m, is a good example. This high ridge reflects the outcrop of the Roeburndale Grit in the centre of a
fairly gentle anticline, the dips of which are not quite so steep as
those of the hill slopes. The valley to the south lies along a shale
outcrop in a gentle syncline. In the area north of Littledale Fell
grits outcropping in anticlinal areas also give rise to higher ground
and some of the valleys are fault guided. The alternation of resistant sandstone and easily eroded shale greatly helps to impose the
structural features on the visible landscape.

To the south, however, the dips steepen to between 30 and 60
degrees and the close control of structure on landscape is lost.
Bowland shales and Lower Carboniferous limestone are brought
to the surface in the steeply dipping Sykes anticline. In this area,
to the south of the Trough of Bowland [623530], the valleys tend
to cut across the structures, although there is some adjustment to
structure, with the more resistant grits forming the higher ground.
On the whole the flatter areas tend to correspond with outcrops
of harder sandstones, and this must be borne in mind when interpreting the significance of these flatter elements of the landscape.

The Forest of Bowland lies to the south of the great series of
faults that separates the Craven Lowlands from the Craven Highlands. The land to the south has had a tendency to subside, so
that the shales and sandstones of the higher zones of the Carboniferous are thicker here than in the more stable massif to the
north. Between the basin and the massif areas the small, but
interesting, relief forms of the reef knolls are found. These are
closely related to the characteristics of the limestone of which
they are formed, and appear as steep-sided, rounded hills, well
developed in the neighbourhood of Cracoe (980600) (W.W. Black
1958).

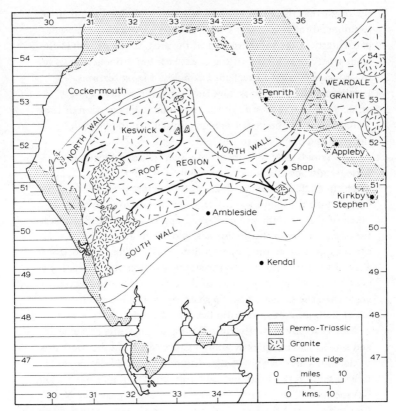

Fig. 1.5 The exposed and inferred unexposed granite beneath northwest England, indicating the connection between the Lake District granite and the Weardale granite. (After Bott 1974.)

The Askrigg block The relatively rigid massif of the Askrigg block is clearly demarcated on its western and southwestern boundaries by the important system of faults, including the Dent fault, the Barbon fault and the Craven faults mentioned above, (see fig. 1.2). At the eastern boundary the rocks of the block dip gently eastwards beneath more recent formations and to the north the structural sag of the Stainmore depression separates the Askrigg block from the adjacent Alston block.

This area has remained relatively stable for a long period with

the result that the Carboniferous sedimentation has been relatively thin, and rocks of lower Carboniferous age are now exposed,
particularly in the southern part of the area. In the Craven Highlands where the outcrop of the Great Scar limestone is extensive,
this rock gives rise to excellent examples of karst features.
Further north in the Yorkshire Dales area the scenery closely
reflects the characteristics of the rhythmic sedimentation of the
Yoredale Series, the massif facies equivalent to the Bowland
shales of the basin area to the south.

The Yoredale Series consists of a succession of limestone,
shale, sandstone and sometimes a thin coal seam, repeated about
seven times. The sequence thickens to the north. These strata of
very varying resistance to erosion lie fairly horizontally over
much of the area, and give rise to a stepped landscape. Steep scars
form, especially on the limestones, and the hill-tops are flat,
often capped by an outcrop of Millstone Grit. The near horizont-
ality of the rocks testifies to the stability of the block area. However, the rocks dip very gently to the east at a slightly greater
angle than the surface. The dip steepens in this direction as the
lower Carboniferous rocks dip beneath the more recent strata.

The strata are abruptly cut off along major faults to the west
and south. The complex system of Craven faults in the southwest
of the block area have moved at different times. The Middle
Craven fault in the south moved during the Carboniferous period,
but the Inner Craven fault and its northern extension, the North
Craven fault, and the Dent fault further north, moved during the
post-Carboniferous - pre-Mesozoic earth movements, with both
vertical and lateral displacement. The latter movement is thought
to have been partially responsible for the joint pattern of the
Great Scar limestone (Wager 1931; Moseley & Ahmed 1967).
Small inliers of lower Palaeozoic and pre-Cambrian basement
rocks outcrop beneath the limestone north of the North Craven
fault in the Greta valley and south of Horton in Ribblesdale and
Malham Tarn. The throw was down to the west in the south along
the Craven fault but to the east along the Dent fault. The South
Craven fault and its extension, the Outer Craven fault, have
moved more recently, probably in later Tertiary times. The fault-
line scarps form visible features in the landscape, for example at

Giggleswick Scar near Settle, [800658] owing to the juxta-
position of rocks of differing resistance (Clayton 1966).

The Alston block The characteristics of the Alston block closely
resemble those of the Askrigg block to the south from the
structural and scenic points of view, although there are some
minor differences of interest. Like the Askrigg block, the Alston
block has a well-marked and faulted western boundary, which is
continued on the north side, matching the southern fault boundary of the Askrigg block. Similarly the Alston block sinks gently
eastwards beneath the younger strata. The boundary between the
two blocks is formed by the Stainmore gap, which is both a topographic and structural depression.

The faults forming the western margin of the Alston block,
like those to the south, are complex, The important Pennine
faults include an inner, middle and outer fault line, which have
moved at different stages in the development of the area. The
Inner and Middle Pennine faults moved during the Hercynian
earth movements and part of the Lower Palaeozoic succession
has been brought to the surface, forming the Cross Fell inlier.
This gives rise to the conical hills of Dufton and Murton Pikes
[700266] and [735231]. The northern faults are the North and
South Stublick dislocations, which again moved at different
times. Movements along the Outer Pennine fault and North Stublick fault have been much more recent. These movements have
given rise to the great faulted scarp bounding the western margin
of the Alston block, where the newer rocks of the Eden valley
have been recently, possibly during the early Pleistocene, down-
faulted against the Carboniferous rocks of the Alston block.

Another minor element of the landscape of the Alston block,
which differentiates it from the Askrigg block, is the outcrop of
the Whin Sill, which is a Carboniferous dolerite. This resistant
material forms the crags of High Cup Nick [745263] and outcrops in the upper part of the waterfall of High Force in Teesdale
[800284]. The blocks owe some of their characteristics to their
deeper seated structure.

Recent gravity and magnetic surveys (M.H.P. Bott 1967) have
revealed the Devonian Weardale granite in the basement rocks

beneath the Alston block, while the central part of the Askrigg
block is underlain by the Wensleydale granite. The basement
rocks are at shallow depths beneath the blocks, but sink deeper
as the Carboniferous rocks thicken along the hinge lines such as
the Stublick fault in the north, the Lunesdale-Butterknowle fault
line, associated with the Cotherstone and Stainmore trough,
between the blocks, and the Craven fault belt in the south. These
basement granites have exerted a strong control on the faulting in
the area, while the incipient jointing of the granites has allowed
mineralisation to take place locally. The mineralisation occurred
100 million years after the emplacement of the granite and so
cannot be directly related to it, despite the close areal correlation
of granite and mineralisation.

Uplift can be accounted for by the tendency to isostatic
adjustment of the relatively low density granites. The importance
of this in the surface relief is commented upon later. G.A.L.
Johnson (1967) also draws attention to the importance of the
buried granites in accounting for areas of uplift in Northern
England. Greater thicknesses of Carboniferous sediments accumulated in the basin areas around these zones of uplift. The basement movements may have controlled the Yoredale cyclothems
and reef knoll distribution. The block areas include the Lake
District, Askrigg and Alston blocks and the Southern Uplands of
Scotland massif, which covers the Cheviot area; the Northumberland trough separates the last two areas.

The northern Pennines The Stublick faults, which are followed by
the Tyne valley, demarcate the boundary between the Alston block
and the most northerly part of the Pennines. There is a change in
the scenery of the northern Pennines, particularly when compared
with the Craven Highland, due to a change in the lithology of the
lower Carboniferous rocks as they are followed northwards. The
limestones virtually die out in the north and their place is taken
by sandstones and shales, so that limestone scenery becomes less
conspicuous northwards until it virtually disappears north of the
Tyne valley. However, a few thin bands of limestone still occur in
the upper part of the Northumbrian Carboniferous strata.

The strata of the northern Pennines consist of the Cementstone group at the base of the series, including some volcanic strata near the Tweed. Above this lies the Fell sandstone group, the massive members of which exert a considerable control on the relief. These rocks are the quivalent of the Millstone Grit further south. The Scremerston Coal group, of estuarine or fresh-water character, is similar to the Cementstone rocks with the addition of thin coal seams. Even the uppermost limestone group consists mainly of sandstones and shales, but a few thin limestone bands occur reaching 15 m to 18 m in thickness. One of these, the Great limestone, is very persistent and can be traced south to correlate with the Main limestone of the Alston and Askrigg blocks.

The scenery of this area is also diversified by the outcrop of the Whin Sill, which forms the well-known bold north-facing scarp, followed along its crest by the Roman Wall north of the Tyne valley. The sill runs out to sea in cliffs at Bambrough [180350] and outcrops in the Farne Islands offshore.

The Fell sandstone forms bold scarps throughout North-umberland north of the Tyne. They are arranged in arcuate form around the Cheviot massif and the Bewcastle Fells to the west; from both of these areas the rocks dip outwards. In the area to the east of the Cheviots the continuity of the scarps is broken by northeast to southwest faults. To the south of the Whin Sill scarp a limestone bed forms a strong scarp to the south of the dolerite one, both presenting steep faces to the north. Upper Redesdale lies in a tectonic depression.

Lower Palaeozoic Uplands

The Cheviot Hills Igneous rocks form an important element in some of the Lower Palaeozoic areas of Northern England, and the Cheviot Hills exemplify this well. The rocks forming these hills are largely Devonian in age. The roughly circular outcrop of the volcanic rocks has been so deeply denuded that an intrusion of granite in its centre has been laid bare by erosion. The volcanic rocks consist of coarse ashes and agglomerates at the base, over-lain by vast outpourings of andesitic lava. The central outcrop of granite in the Cheviot Hills is a replacement in the main vent.

There are also many dykes in the area, which often form minor relief features and bring variety to the generally bleak open ground of steep rounded hills typical of the igneous rocks of the Cheviots. The dyke swarms are aligned north-north-west to south-south-east and north-north-east to south-south-west. They cut through the lavas as well as the granite and are particularly numerous on the southern part of the granite outcrop. The granite on the whole forms the higher ground, but this is not always so, and the grey rocks of its aureole are also resistant and form high ground. The lavas are of different resistance and some of the relief reflects this variation, while fault lines on the southern and northern margins of the igneous area are responsible for fault-line scarp features. These tend to give the Cheviot Hills a horst-like appearance when viewed from the east (Common 1954).

The Lake District The rocks of the Lake District play a large part in determining its character, and in distinguishing it from the surrounding areas. The district is an elongated structural dome in which the Lower Palaeozoic rocks outcrop within a ring of younger Carboniferous strata (Marr 1916). The rocks are of three types, giving three belts running eastwest across the area. To the north the oldest rocks, the Skiddaw slates of lower Ordovician age, outcrop. In the centre the Borrowdale Volcanic Series form the rugged country characteristic of the central Lake District hills, while to the south the Silurian strata give another belt of rather more subdued and lower relief. Within the area a number of igneous intrusions outcrop, such as the Ennerdale granophyre and Eskdale granite on the west and the smaller area of Shap granite in the east.

The Skiddaw slates are very contorted and cleaved, and act as relatively homogenous strata as far as landscape formation is concerned. The hills formed of these rocks are steep, smooth and on the whole rounded. There is a small outcrop of the Skiddaw slates in the southwest of the area, forming the mountain of Black Combe [135855], where these rocks outcrop along an anticlinal axis. The relationship of the overlying Borrowdale Volcanic rocks to the Skiddaw slates is a matter of doubt, although there is increasing evidence that the two series are conformable in some places. In other areas there has probably been faulting along the bedding planes.

The Borrowdale Volcanic Series is largely pyroclastic volcanic in type, ranging from fine tuffs to coarse agglomerates, but there are also many inter-bedded lava flows of variable character. Some are basalts and others are rhyolitic although andesites are the most common. The strata are discontinuous and vary in their resistance to denudation. This is important in accounting for the relief of the central Lake District, where the landscape is knobbly in detail, particularly in the areas where the harder members of the series outcrop. Some of the tuffs have the character of welded tuffs or ignimbrites and often show some form of columnar structure. The bulk of the rocks were probably extruded sub-aerially, but they have been very considerably modified since their formation by solfataric and metamorphic processes. The total thickness of the Borrowdale Volcanic Series probably exceeds 3000 m in places.

The Volcanic Series is overlain unconformably by the Coniston Limestone Series, which outcrops in a narrow belt between the volcanic rocks and the Silurian rocks to the south. The strata include some limestone, although the lowest bed is a conglomerate, and there are also shales and volcanic strata. The outcrop is too thin, however, to have a very marked effect on the relief.

The succeeding Silurian Series play a more important part in forming the characteristic relief of the southern Lake District and the neighbouring unit, the Howgill Fells. The beds consist of shales, flags and in the higher strata some grits. Some of the rocks consist of alternating mudstones and gritty silts, which show graded bedding. These rocks are relatively homogenous and produce smooth slopes by comparison with the rocky and knobbly relief of the Borrowdale Volcanic Series. The relief developed on the Silurian rocks is, however, similar to that of the Skiddaw slate areas.

The Caledonian earth movements were responsible for the main characteristics of the Lake District structure. The rocks were folded to give the present southwest or west-south-westerly trend to the alignments in the Lake District. The Skiddaw slates received their tight folding during this Devonian upheaval and much faulting also took place. The major axis of uplift lay along the present outcrop of the Skiddaw slates and accounts for the exposure of the oldest rocks in this area. The relatively weak shales of the Silurian were also heavily folded. Both these rock groups now act as relatively homogenous strata, on account of these intense earth movements, which have precluded structural control exerting much influence in the area of their outcrop. The Borrowdale Volcanic Series were more massive and resistant and were in general less severely folded.

The Howgill Fells Structurally the Howgill Fells form an outlying part of the Lake District but they are a distinct unit topographically. In most of this triangular stretch of country Silurian rocks outcrop, although there are small areas of Ordovician rocks in the east (Marr and Fearnsides 1909; Ingham 1966). What has been said of the Silurian rocks of the Lake District applies also to those of the Howgill Fells, which form an eastern extension of the Lake District, lying east of the Lune valley. The gorge of this river, south of Tebay [620040], separates the Howgill Fells from the main high ground of the Lake District.

Both these upland tracts probably owe their present elevation to recent uplift during the Tertiary period and not to the earth movements of the earlier orogenic upheavals. Evidence for this view is considered on p. 47. The Lake District was uplifted first during the Caledonian orogeny, secondly during the post-Carboniferous period and most recently during the Tertiary. The Howgill Fells were also uplifted along an eastwest axis in the Tertiary. period, forming a monoclinal block with a steep southern slope and a gentle northern one. At the northern margin the Silurian rocks disappear beneath an unconformable cover of younger Carboniferous strata. The eastern boundary of the Howgill Fells is formed by the Dent fault, along which the Carboniferous strata on the east were let down against the Silurian rocks on the west. Along this fault line the Howgill Fells come into contact with the Askrigg block, and the contrast between the structurally controlled landscape of the Askrigg block and the smooth slopes of the homogenous rocks of the Howgill Fells can most readily be appreciated. Movement along the Dent fault has not taken place during the Tertiary, but it forms a line of weakness that has been in part exploited by streams and ice thus forming both a structural and relief boundary to the Howgill Fells.

The centre and south of the Isle of Man The Isle of Man can be broadly divided into two parts. The northern lowland part is considered later. The centre and south of the island is a highland zone which is connected with the northern Lake District by an underwater ridge running from Ramsey to Whitehaven in a southwest to northeast direction. This has been revealed by gravity observations made by Bott (1964) in the northeast Irish Sea. The high ground of the island consists mainly of Manx slates. The exact age of these rocks is in some doubt, although they were thought by Lamplugh to belong to the equivalent of the lowest part of the Skiddaw slates. They are now usually referred to the Cambrian period, so that, with the exception of the Ingletonian rocks which are thought to be pre-Cambrian, they appear to represent the oldest rocks outcropping in Northern England. The Manx slates have been intensely compressed and include strata termed grits and flags as well as slates. In places they have suffered much disturbance and have been converted into crush conglomerates or fault breccias. On the whole their effect on the landscape is similar to that of the Skiddaw slates, though structural control is not so strong due to the homogeneity of the rocks and their very complex structures. The hill slopes, therefore, are relatively smooth and stages of denudation are fairly conspicuous in the present landscape.

There are one or two small intrusions of granite into the Manx slates, forming the Foxdale [270770] and Dhoon outcrops along the central stratigraphical axis of the island. A number of short dykes, nearly all of which trend northeast to southwest, have been intruded along the strike of the Manx slates. The slates must have been folded and crushed before the dyke intrusion and the emplacement of the granites, but there has also been subsequent further crushing which has affected the dykes. The granites and dykes were intruded before the Carboniferous period, although a later series of dykes in the southwest may be Tertiary in age.

The fringing scarps and lowlands

In the lower areas there are also two groups of country with a distinction similar to that of the uplands. There are those areas fringing the uplands where younger strata dip off the older structural units and give rise to a series of fringing scarps. There are also the contrasting areas where the solid rocks are hidden beneath a later drift surface, so that the solid strata play little direct part in the visible relief. Drift often covers other parts of the landscape as well, but it is only sufficiently thick and extensive to form the dominant element of the relief in a few lowland areas. However, drift also dominates the landscape in some of the valleys within the upland areas, as will be discussed later.

Carboniferous fringing scarps

Fringing scarp of the Lake District Apart from the western side of the Lake District, the older rocks of this area are surrounded by a fringe of Carboniferous rocks. The scarp form of this fringe is best developed on the north, northeast and southeast of the Lake District. On the west the Carboniferous is overlapped by the New Red sandstone which rests directly against the older rocks. The structural attitude of these fringing rocks gives some useful evidence of the later earth movements that have affected the older core areas. The earliest rock of the post-Silurian period is the basal conglomerate, once thought to be Carboniferous, but now considered more likely to belong to the Devonian. This very coarse conglomerate gives rise to distinctive fells at the northern end of Ullswater in particular and also occurs in the south of the Isle of Man. The character of these conglomerates indicates active erosion of steep slopes before the deposition of the Carboniferous strata.

From the point of view of interpreting the present landscape, the relationship between the dip of the Carboniferous fringe and the older rocks is of great significance. The northward-dipping limestone that lies to the north of the Howgill Fells dips at such an angle that its base would just pass over the present hill tops, suggesting that the gentle northern slopes of the fells may represent a modified sub-Carboniferous surface in part. The pattern of the outcrop of the limestone fringe round the northern Lake District also gives evidence of the form of the dome-shaped uplift of the Lake District. This uplift probably took place in two phases, one before the deposition of the Permian, the evidence for which will be cited later, and one during the Tertiary, when the later rocks were also involved in the movements, (Mitchell 1956).

The fringe on the northeastern side of the Lake District and Howgill Fells consists of the lower strata of the Carboniferous, which in this area is made up of thick beds of pure limestone as well as sandstones. The limestone gives rise to wide areas of limestone pavements, but there does not seem to be much cave formation in this area. Limestone also fringes the southern part of the Lake District. The structure here is less obvious and much of the ground, particularly around Kendal, is drift-covered.

Cheviot fringing scarps Some of the major features of the fringes of the main igneous outcrop of the Cheviots are formed by the outcrop of the resistant Fell sandstone. This forms west-facing scarps along the crests of faulted and asymmetrical anticlines, the northern one runs northsouth, pitching to the north, and the southern one, which replaces it, trends south-south-west (see fig. 1.2). Between these major landscape forming features and the sea there are many other minor dislocations that do not play an important part in the modern landscape. This area merges into the northern Pennines and has already been discussed.

The Durham and Northumberland Coal Measures The Millstone Grit and the Coal Measures of the Upper Carboniferous outcrop in an area lying between the Alston block and the sea. This belt widens southwards and in the area south of the Tyne is separated from the coast by yet another scarp fringe. These upper Carboniferous strata dip gently east and the harder bands form west-facing scarps. The Millstone Grit of this area is unlike that further south, although there are some beds of sandstone, which form the scarps, lying between relatively thick layers of shale. Rather similar rocks continue up into the Coal Measures above, with the addition particularly in the Middle Coal Measures, of valuable coal seams. The gentle easterly dip of the rocks of the exposed coal-field is disturbed by faults in places, many of which trend within 25 degrees of an eastwest direction. This has the effect of making many of the scarp features discontinuous, so that they are not a conspicuous element of the landscape, particularly where shales predominate. These areas form low country, subsequently drift covered. Nevertheless the broad belt of relatively low ground that has developed along the outcrop of the Coal Measures is of importance in the development of the landscape on a broad scale, particularly with regard to the formation of the drainage pattern, which will be considered later.

The Craven Lowlands In the angle between the southern edge of the Askrigg block and the Forest of Bowland, lies a lower area known as the Craven Lowlands. This area forms a link between the Askrigg block and southern Pennines, and is of interest from a structural point of view as it exemplifies the facies of the basins as opposed to those of the block or massif. The basin was an area of subsidence in which much thicker deposits accumulated than those on the block to the north. The Bowland shales in the basin take the place of the Yoredale strata on the block. The area south of the marginal reef knolls is relatively low ground on the softer basin rocks which have been exploited to form the Aire gap. This is a low corridor, linking the Aire and Ribble valleys. The diversion of the upper Aire into the Ribble is associated with glacial action. Much of the present relief of the area is superficially modified by glacial deposits in the form of drumlins.

The Permo-Triassic or New Red sandstone fringing areas There are three major areas where Permian and Triassic rocks form important elements in the landscape. These are, firstly, the Lancashire Plain, secondly in the Eden valley and part of the western Lake District fringe, and thirdly in eastern County Durham, where the Permian Magnesian limestone outcrops between the sea and the Coal Measures, forming a triangular area thinly covered with drift.

The Lancashire Plain The Lancashire Plain, which can be approx-

imately delimited by the 100 m contour, lies between the
Pennines and the Irish Sea. Northwards it merges with the western Lake District fringe. It widens southwards from Lancaster to
reach its maximum width of about 64 km just south of Manchester, which lies near its eastern edge. Southwards it merges
with the Cheshire-Shropshire plain. The area of the plain lying
north of the Mersey is included in this volume. The northern part
is drained by the southern Lake District streams, the Lune, the
Wyre, lower Ribble, to which the river Douglas flows, and the
Mersey. It is appropriate in some sections to refer also to the
Wirral Peninsula, lying between the Dee and Mersey estuaries.

The plain is underlain mainly by Triassic rocks, although Coal
Measures are exposed northeast of Liverpool and underlie much
of south Lancashire. The Coal Measures mainly consist of un-
resistant rocks, but occasional sandstones form small hills. There
is a structural saddle over the inner Mersey Estuary, while a basin
occurs in west Lancashire in which Keuper marl has been
deposited. This rock is found north of Formby Point [268070].
In the saddle area seams of coal up to 3.4 m thick occur in the
Middle Coal Measures, this thickness of coal being the equivalent
of more than 30 m of peat. The total thickness of Coal Measures
near Wigan [580060] and St Helens [510960] is 73 m, increasing
to 1420 m near Manchester.

The Carboniferous rocks were tilted and eroded before the
New Red sandstone was deposited. The lowest Permian stratum
is the Collyhurst sandstone, which has dune bedding. It is 715 m
thick in a borehole at Formby, but only 11 m thick at Skellow
Clough. The sandstone is overlain by the Manchester marls, which
are marine Permian strata. These are followed by the Bunter
Pebble Beds, the Upper Mottled sandstone, Keuper waterstones
and Keuper marl. Around Liverpool the Bunter Pebble Beds are
about 300 m thick, and are desert flood deposits. The Upper Mottled sandstones are current bedded, and reach 168 m thickness in
the Wirral. The Keuper sandstone is hard and less homogeneous,
being less thick in the Wirral than it is at Formby in the basin,
where it is 300 m thick. The overlying Keuper marl is 1000 m
thick in the Cheshire basin, where it includes 244 m of salt.

The strata are disturbed by faulting dating probably from the

Tertiary, although some of the activity could be Cretaceous in age. The relief features formed by faulting were obliterated during the Tertiary, and no longer influence the land forms. The Carboniferous strata are cut off along a fault that runs north-south through Bickerstaffe [445042] and Burscough [435107], where it joins another fault trending to the northeast, which also cuts off the Carboniferous strata. The continuation of the boundary fault runs south-south-east, as the Frodsham fault, to cross the Mersey estuary near Runcorn [495816]. The throw along the major fault exceeds 300 m. Various other smaller faults cut both the Carboniferous and Triassic rocks, causing offsetting of the sub-drift outcrops. Although some of these faults also have large throws, that near Melling [390002] having a throw of over 300 m, they rarely affect the relief.

The main relief forming rocks are the Keuper Basement Beds, which are rather more resistant than the other Triassic strata. In some areas however, Bunter forms the higher ground, for example in the higher parts of Liverpool [415865] and Thurstaston Hill [245846] in Wirral. The highest ground in the Lancashire plain, however, occurs on the more resistant Carboniferous strata. In particular the hills of Parbold [515127], Ashurst's Beacon [501078], and Billinge Hill [525014] are all on the Carboniferous, reaching heights of 153 m, 168 m and 179 m, respectively.

The Dee estuary is outlined by faults, both of which throw down to the east, with Coal Measures outcropping on the west and under the estuary, and Triassic rocks on the east, where the Bunter Pebble Beds outcrop. It is not, therefore, a rift valley form. The Mersey owes relatively little of its configuration to faulting.

The Lancashire plain continues northwards into the Fylde, which is drained by the Wyre and lies between the Ribble and Lune estuaries. The area is underlain by Triassic rocks, but these rarely outcrop at the surface. Bunter occurs in the east and Keuper in the west. Again there is no surface trace of faulting in the area. Most of the rock surface lies below sea level, normally between − 12 and − 30 m, increasing in places to nearly − 37 m.

The Eden valley and western Lake District fringe On either side

of the Lake District a belt of Permian Brockram occurs, this is
deposit consisting mainly of angular chips of Carboniferous limestone, set in a pinkish matrix. The Brockram in the Appleby area
came from the north, the material being eroded from the rising
Pennine fault scarp. Near Kirkby Stephen the Brockram is
thicker, the Stenkrith Brockram of this area being 18 m thick. It
was derived from the limestones, which were already folded,
6.5-8 km south of its present position. The material shows
imbrication and is a water-laid fan deposit. It is a hard calcareous
rock in which well-developed potholes have formed in the bed of
the river Eden at Kirkby Stephen [772075]. The distribution of
the Brockram shows that the Eden valley was a low lying area
already during this period, which is contemporaneous with the
Penrith sandstone. Brockram also occurs on the western side of
the Lake District in west Cumberland and Furness and to a
limited extent in the south of the Isle of Man and around Peel on
the west. In the Eden valley the Brockram is thick and resistant
enough to cause a steepening of the river gradient where it outcrops across the Eden near Kirkby Stephen.

The succeeding member of the New Red sandstone, the Penrith sandstone, forms a well-marked northsouth scarp on the west
of the Eden valley north of Penrith. This is a coarse red rock,
often formed of millet-seed grains, and in places brockrams occur
between the lower and upper members of the series. The Penrith
sandstone only outcrops in the Eden valley, where it is an important element in the landscape and reaches 300 m in thickness.
This sandstone must have accumulated in an arid area on account
of the roundness of its grains, but it is mostly found as a water-
laid deposit. The rock is not equally resistant everywhere. It is
weak and crumbly near Appleby, but northwards the cemen-
tation of the rock becomes stronger, until near Penrith it is both
a good building stone and an important landscape forming rock.
The cement that binds the rock is siliceous.

There must have been high ground to the south to form these
rocks, so that even at this time the Eden valley must have been a
negative area. This characteristic was renewed during the movement along the outer Pennine fault during the Tertiary, when the
Permo-Triassic rocks were let down against the Carboniferous on

the western downthrow side of the fault. The accumulation of the lower members of the New Red sandstone series in the Vale of Eden may have been due to early movement along the Pennine fault system.

The upper members of the New Red sandstone strata consist of the St Bees shales, with gypsum, and the thicker and more important St Bees sandstone. The former may in fact be upper Permian marls. The St Bees sandstone is a fine-grained rock, compared with the Penrith sandstone, and it has less well-rounded grains. It is on the whole less resistant throughout its outcrop with the result that it does not form such conspicuous features as the Penrith sandstone scarp north of Penrith. The main outcrops of the St Bees sandstone are between the river Eden and the Pennine faults on the east and along the coast at and south of St Bees Head on the west. In these areas the rock is also largely covered by drift, so that it does not play so direct a part in the landscape as the more resistant rocks.

East Durham Plateau The Magnesian limestone outcrops on the East Durham Plateau in a wedge-shaped area, and has a well marked west-facing scarp rising above the Coal Measure shales to the west. The rocks reach the coast as vertical cliffs on the east. They are thinly bedded, creamy-white limestones, which are relatively resistant and form good water-bearing strata, although the water is very hard. The rocks are variable and of interest geologically, but the variations do not play a very important part in the landscape. The rocks on the whole dip rather more steeply than the surface of the plateau, so that successively younger beds outcrop towards the coast. The fairly resistant lower limestone forms the scarp on the western side of the outcrop.

The Solway Lowland The Solway Lowlands, although underlain by Triassic and some Jurassic deposits at depth, are thickly covered by glacial till and more recent deposits of various types. These lowlands merge into a great belt of glacial deposits that stretches up into the Eden valley, as already mentioned, and along the Tyne gap, and around the western fringes of the Lake District. The character of these deposits will be considered later

in connection with glacial features. In this area the control of
solid rock on the relief is negligible.

The north of the Isle of Man In the northern part of the Isle of
Man the solid rocks are so deeply covered by glacial deposits and
later sediments that their character is only known in the relatively
few deep bores that have penetrated to them. There is a sharp
boundary between the high ground of the Manx slates to the
south and lower ground to the north. The lowland is by no means
devoid of relief, but this is not dependent on the solid rocks.

In many other parts of the region not included in these last
two areas, the upland and the lowlands are partially modified by
more recent deposits. These veil the underlying strata partially,
but do not obliterate their significance in the landscape. Thus in
many areas the valley bottoms may be covered by drift of various
types and even the hill tops may be buried beneath a blanket of
thick peat, yet the imprint of the rocks is present. It is the presence of grits or shales as opposed to limestone, for example, that
allows the peat to form on the higher moors. The rock type, therefore, is reflected in the superficial cover even though it may be
buried by it. The vegetation and the stone walls often give a clue
to the underlying rocks, where these are not visibly exposed on
the surface.

The differentiation of Northern England
Factor analysis has been used as an objective method of charac-
terising different parts of Northern England, in terms of readily
measurable variables, obtained from O.S. map data. The intercor-
relations of the ten variables are given in the table (p.200) for the
six different areas analysed. The areas were each divided into
twenty 25 km^2 subsections. They are the Askrigg block, the
Alston block, the Cheviots, the Lake District, the Solway lowland
and the Northumberland coastal strip. The relief variables intercor-
relate highly apart from the Askrigg and Alston block data, a
result due to the plateau nature of these two areas, which are relatively little dissected compared with the other highland areas.

The factor loadings indicate which variables are most important in differentiating the areas. The absolute relief loads most

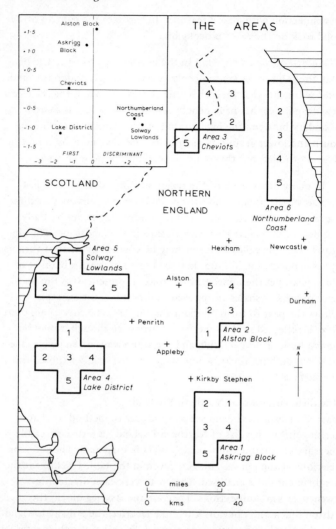

Fig. 1.6 *Above* *a)* The areas used for factor analysis. Each area covers 20 units of 25 km² each. The inset shows the position of the centroids of the 20 units for each area, based on multiple discriminant analysis, using the first four factor scores for the 20 units of each area. *Opposite* *b)* The factor 1 and factor 2 scores plotted against each other for the 20 units for each area. The six areas are differentiated by different symbols.

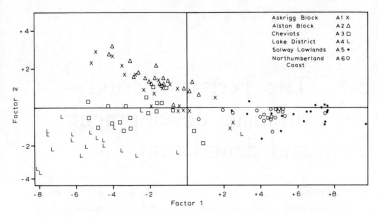

highly on the first factor, while drainage variables load most
highly on the second factor for all the areas combined.

The distinction between the areas can be assessed by plotting
factor 1 against factor 2, as shown on fig. 1.6. The Lake District
forms a compact group at the opposite end of the factor 1 axis
to the lowland areas, while factor 2 differentiates the Lake
District from the Pennine and Cheviot areas, largely in terms of
the drainage variables and summit dissection. The two Pennine
blocks are shown to be very similar in their characteristics. This
method provides a quantitative means of assessing the differences within and between the six areas analysed.

In order to test the significance of the differences between
the six areas, the first four factor loadings on the 120 small subsections were used in multiple discriminant analysis. The results
showed that the first factor loading explained 76.4% of the total
variance and the second factor a further 20.13%, while the contribution of the 3rd and 4th factors was very small, being 3.43%
and 0.02% respectively. The F value, which indicates whether the
discriminant functions can successfully distinguish between the
six groups, is 3.11. This value is significant at the 97.5% level of
confidence. When the centroids of the six groups for the first
two discriminant functions are plotted against each other the
resulting pattern closely resemble the plot of the first and second
factor scores. This is because these two factors together provide
96.6% of the discriminatory power.

2 The Tertiary period – drainage development and denudation

No solid rocks younger than Triassic outcrop at the surface in Northern England, although a small area of Jurassic rocks is buried beneath the drift of the Solway Lowlands. The development of the landscape during the Tertiary period must be worked out as far as is possible from the evidence of the landforms by geomorphological techniques. The drainage pattern and the relics of erosional features related to former base-levels provide the best information for this purpose. It is difficult to separate these two methods of approach in reaching conclusions concerning the landscape development, but for clarity of description the drainage development will be considered first.

Drainage development
The present drainage pattern (fig. 1.1) reflects the broad structrual features of the districts that have been mentioned in the preceding chapter. The areas of high ground naturally form the source areas from which the major drainage lines flow to the coast. Two areas have a modified radial system of drainage, that of the Cheviot igneous area being the best developed, while the drainage pattern of the Lake District is related more to an elongated eastwest watershed and is not really truly radial in character. The appearance of radial drainage is made more apparent by the pattern of the lakes, which Linton (1957) has shown to be related to radial glacial outflow and erosion.

The streams draining the Pennine blocks flow in general eastward, from the Coquet and Tyne in the north to the Ure and Aire in the south, although the more southerly streams, such as the Wharfe, Aire and Ribble have a southerly component at least in their upper reaches.

The other rivers of importance in the area are the Eden and the Lune. The former is closely related to the down-faulted trough west of the Pennine faults, and the Lune, which has had a complex history, flows south, after draining the major part of the Howgill Fells, to reach the sea at Lancaster. The longer rivers, with the exception of the Eden and Lune, flow in gentler courses to the North Sea. The rivers flowing west to the Irish Sea are shorter and steeper on the whole.

Although many of the streams follow major structural elements, most of them are not clearly related to the underlying rocks over which they flow. Sissons (1960) has drawn attention to the great number of discordant streams in Northern England. This characteristic of the drainage pattern can be explained in a number of ways. One or two of these possibilities will be mentioned and the one which appears best to account for the present landscape can be adopted as a working hypothesis. So much of the evidence has been lost by glacial modification and earlier denudation that it may never be possible to ascertain without doubt the Tertiary pattern of drainage development in the area.

(1) One possible method of landscape development is that suggested by Sissons. He considered that denudation during the Tertiary reduced the area to low relief by subaerial erosion. This landscape, perhaps with some residual eminences, is thought to have been submerged beneath the sea, accompanied by warping and faulting. The drowned landscape then slowly emerged by stages in the late Tertiary. As the land emerged the drainage lines were extended across a veneer of marine sediments. There is now no trace of these sediments, but this is not an insuperable objection to the hypothesis. This method of development would account for the discordance of many of the streams and the presence of marine erosion surfaces around the main upland blocks of country.

There are, however, difficulties in accepting a view that implies lowering of sea-level by about 1000 m to allow the emergence of the present hills during the later part of the Tertiary period, following an earlier rise of sea-level to drown the landscape. Some of these problems and further implications of this type of development have been commented upon by Linton (1964).

(2) Nevertheless the point that discordance of streams suggests epigenesis is a valid one, and one which has been used by those who have put forward different views of the drainage development. An alternative hypothesis is Linton's which suggests that the drainage was initiated on a cover of Cretaceous rocks as these emerged from beneath the sea in early Tertiary time. He has suggested that such a surface sloped roughly eastwards over most of the country, with a short steep gradient to the west. This sloping surface could account for many of the main easterly-flowing streams, such as the Tyne, Tees and Ure, but it does not account well for many of the other streams such as the Eden, Lune, upper Ribble and Aire, nor for the radial drainage of the Cheviot area and the elongated radial drainage of the Lake District. By requiring superimposition, this theory, however, also accounts for the discordant streams. It is clear that the original pattern has suffered considerable modification by subsequent development and stream capture.

The question of the former extent of Mesozoic rocks over the area is a difficult but relevant one. There is no direct evidence of their former presence and the fact that some of the major upland areas of the district have been relatively stable and upstanding throughout long periods of geological time suggests that this trend may have continued during the Mesozoic. If this were so, then it would not be expected that the Mesozoic cover would have ever been very thick, and it may not have covered all the upland area. On the whole it seems probable that there was at least a thin cover of Mesozoic rocks on which the early Tertiary drainage pattern developed. The Alston block, according to Trotter (1929a), was actually depressed during the Hercynian earth movements relative to the Lake District-Howgill Fell axis of uplift to the south and the Bewcastle uplift to the north. Therefore it seems likely that this part at least may have been low enough to receive Mesozoic sediments, which Trotter considers may have been about 1225-1525 m thick.

(3) The hypothesis put forward by Trotter to account for the

drainage pattern of the Alston block is probably applicable also to much of Northern England. The earliest pattern that can be reconstructed in the Alston block consists of easterly flowing streams consequent upon the early Tertiary uplift of the Mesozoic cover. These streams flowed east from the Pennine fault line at right angles across the then buried Permian scarp, following the dip of these strata on which they were conformable. A similar easterly-flowing pattern can be discerned on the northern part of the Askrigg block. In the southern part, however, the general slope of the surface on which the streams were developed appears to have been directed more to the south, towards the subsiding area of the Craven Lowlands beyond the south Craven fault at the southern boundary of the Askrigg block. Further north, in the northern Pennines, a similar pattern can be discerned north of the Tyne and south of the Cheviot igneous area. The early Tertiary uplift of the Lake District-Howgill Fell axis was also important in initiating the drainage pattern of this area, which to the north flowed northeast into the down-warped Eden valley drainage.

The work of this early pattern of rivers would have reduced the landscape to fairly low relief by denudation, producing a peneplain by mid-Tertiary times. Later earth movements in Plio-Pleistocene times may have warped and uplifted the old peneplain mainly along the earlier directions, although in places these later earth-movements appear to have resulted in modifications of the drainage pattern. The streams of the Alston block show very clearly their close relationship to the uplift and warping of this Tertiary erosion surface, which in this area is closely related to the structure of the Carboniferous rocks. This relationship is supported by the trend surface analysis discussed later.

Throughout the period of development, however, the drainage pattern has been modified by capture. This has been partly caused by subsequent development along the outcrops of weaker strata. The east-flowing rivers in Northumberland are a much-quoted example of this process. Another important influence has been the operation of the law of unequal slopes, acting in favour of the shorter, steeper streams, flowing to the west in many instances.

As a working hypothesis it may be suggested that the drainage was initiated in the early Tertiary on an uplifted surface covered by Mesozoic sediments, the form of which was broadly coincident with the present pattern of highland and lowland. Erosion produced a peneplain during the earlier part of the Tertiary period. This surface was warped and uplifted along some of the major fault lines of the area, repeating earlier uplifts to form the essentials of the present relief of early Pleistocene times. The warping of this surface, modified the drainage pattern.

It is not possible to describe in detail the drainage development throughout the area, but sample areas will be taken to illustrate details of the broad pattern already outlined. The areas that will be described are the Alston block, as worked out by Trotter (1929a), the Howgill Fells and upper Eden drainage, part of this area having been described by Hollingworth (1929) and the eastern Cheviot region, which has been described by Common (1954).

Alston block The original drainage on the Alston block was probably initiated on the emerging Mesozoic cover rocks which were tilted eastwards, thus these early streams flowed east from the line of the Pennine faults as shown on fig. 2.1. Relics of these streams include the easterly-flowing part of the North Tyne and the upper part of the river Pont and Seaton Burn, all three being relics of a once continuous stream (fig. 2.1). The major part of the river Tyne, the upper Derwent and parts of the Wear, Gaunless and Greta also probably represent remnants of former consequent streams. These easterly flowing streams helped to produce the peneplain which has subsequently been warped, faulted and uplifted, and which is even now very conspicuous in the landscape.

The east-flowing consequents must have become disrupted during the formation of the peneplain by subsequent stream formation and capture. The Wear shows this very clearly. The stream is formed of three eastwest sections linked by two northsouth sections upstream of Bishop Auckland. Where this type of adjustment is not accompanied by notches in the peneplain there is evidence that the captures took place during the formation of the peneplain. There are, however, later captures of a similar type that took place after the peneplain had been uplifted in the late Tertiary or early Pleistocene movements.

These later earth-movements produced the present form of the Alston block and also caused some modification of the drainage pattern. Their effect is particularly clearly seen in the neighbourhood of the Teesdale anticline, which was formed during these latest earth movements. The trend surface analysis supports the relationship between streams and surface, (see.p.51,52). Trotter has shown how closely the relief and structure are associated in this area, the present streams having been modified to flow down the limbs of the anticline in northsouth courses. Examples of these streams include the southeasterly flowing tributaries of the upper

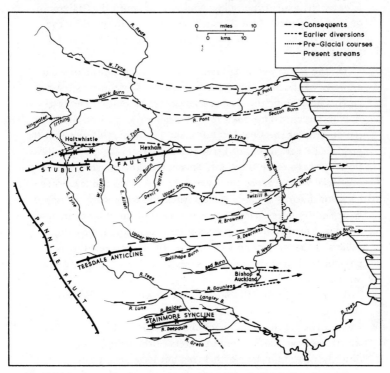

Fig. 2.1 Drainage development in the Alston block. (Based largely on the work of the F.M. Trotter.)

Tees, while on the northern limb of the east-west anticline the longer streams of the South Tyne tributaries, the west and east Allen and the Devil's Water flow north with the gentle dip of the strata, parallel to the slope of the warped peneplain. The elevation of the peneplain along the lines of the Inner Pennine fault and the North Stublick fault to west and north respectively also resulted in rejuvenation. This caused a later series of captures due to the incision of subsequent streams.

The major tectonic depressions, formed or reformed as a result of the later Tertiary movements, have also become important lines of drainage. On the west the Eden flows in the faulted syncline of the Eden valley depression, while the faulted syncline on the north of the Alston block is followed by the South Tyne and later by the main Tyne valley, while to the south the Stainmore depression, south of the Teesdale anticline, is followed by the drainage of the Lune, Balder and Greta, all of which flow east into the Tees.

On the easterly sloping surface of the peneplain the original drainage has become disrupted by capture, subsequent streams cutting back along the weaker shale bands to capture the east-flowing streams. The major belt of weaker rocks corresponds to the outcrop of the Coal-Measures, and it is along this belt that the preglacial Wear cut back to truncate the streams that originally flowed east to reach the coast. This north-flowing stretch of the preglacial Wear reached the Tyne near Newcastle and it worked back southwards as far as Bishop Auckland to capture the upper Wear and Gaunless. The west-facing scarp of the Magnesian limestone was formed by this process. Its crest is notched by the valleys of the streams now left dry by these captures. It is not possible to deal with all the captures but some of them are shown on fig. 2.1.

In preglacial times the South Tyne flowed to the west to join the Eden as a result of capture by a more vigorous west-flowing stream. The capture took place about a mile southwest of Halt-whistle (see fig. 4.8). The head waters of the Irthing originally flowed east to join the North Tyne, but have been captured by the more vigorous lower Irthing. This river now flows east in its upper reaches then it turns south and finally west and southwest to join the Eden, flowing to the west coast. The law of unequal slopes has, therefore, been operating to move the original watershed further east, as a result of capture of previously east-flowing streams. This has been achieved partly by capture as in the case of the Irthing, and partly by headward extension of the west-flowing streams into the Pennine Fault scarp, where the streams have a very steep gradient.

Howgill Fells and upper Eden valley Similar forces have been at work in the drainage development of the Howgill Fells, involving the upper Eden, the headwaters of the Lune and the east-flowing river Ure. Possible stages in this development, part of which has been discussed by Hollingworth (1929) and McConnell (1939), are indicated in fig. 2.2. The original pattern reflects the character of the early Tertiary deformation of the surface, a movement that was probably renewed along similar lines in the later Tertiary, although there is no evidence of the later warping that has been described on the Alston block. Thus the earliest pattern of which there is clear evidence consists of a series of fairly gentle north-flowing streams, draining the long gentle northern slope of the Howgill Fells towards the downwarp of the Eden valley, already followed by the Eden trunk stream. These north-flowing streams were probably initiated on a thin layer of cover rocks. These have since been stripped off and the streams now bear little relationship to the underlying Lower Palaeozoic strata. Their former courses are indicated by notches at about 300 m further north in the Carboniferous limestone scarp. At this time the whole of the northern part of the Howgill Fells drained to the north, and the watershed continued across the site of the present Lune gorge to join the Lake District watershed. The present Lune gorge south of Tebay [615045] did not exist at this time (see fig. 2.3). The first stage in the disruption of the northerly drainage of the How-gill Fells took place when an east-flowing subsequent developed along the weaker beds of the Ashfell sandstone within the lower Carboniferous. This stream formed the wide valley in which Sun-biggin Tarn lies and which drained north through the Potts Beck valley to the river Eden.

The most important occurrence in the drainage development

of the Howgill Fells was the breaching of the eastwest watershed south of Tebay by a stream cutting headwards from the south. This stream had the advantage of flowing on the steeper southern slope of the Howgill Fell uplift and was guided by a series of faults to the west of Sedbergh [655920]. A trend surface analysis carried out on 68 summit spot heights in the Howgill Fells and the area immediately to the west across the Lune gorge shows the possible former col at an elevation of about 430 m at a position 1 km west of the junction of Borrow Beck and the Lune [060015]. The trend surface pattern is shown in fig. 2.2(b). The cubic trend surface accounts for 73% of the total sum of squares and is, therefore, a reasonably good fit. The summits of Fell

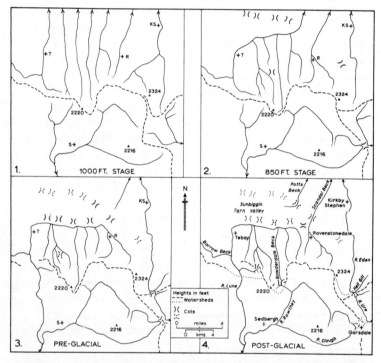

Fig. 2.2 *Above a*) Stages in the drainage development of the Howgill Fells. *Opposite b*) Cubic trend surface of the Howgill Fells summit heights, showing a col at the site of the present Lune Gorge.

Head [647981] and Grayrigg Forest [598998] on either side of
the gorge stand out as residuals of +37 m and +70 m respectively
above the surface. Both are points on the postulated former
watershed. The trend surface analysis thus provides some support
for the hypothesis of watershed breaching in this vicinity to
account for the pattern of the upper Lune drainage.

The breaching of the watershed must have occurred in the
early Pleistocene and it is possible that ice of one of the early
glaciations helped to complete the breach by glacial diffluence,
although no definite evidence is available. The result of the
breaching was to divert first Carlin Gill, then Borrow Beck to the
south-flowing Lune drainage (see figs. 2.2 and 2.3).

When the basal conglomerate was exposed near Tebay rapid
subsequent development eastwards along its outcrop cut off the
drainage to the Sunbiggin Tarn valley. The valley was abandoned
from the west as the present upper Lune extended eastwards to
Ravenstonedale [723040], finally capturing Scandal Beck, part of
the upper waters of the Eden drainage. This stream has, however,
been restored to the Eden as a result of glacial diversion. The
strange pattern of the Lune can be accounted for in this way.
The river flows first north, as Bowderdale Beck, then west and
finally turns south near Tebay, flowing through the impressive
Lune gorge across the former watershed just south of the town
now followed by the M.6 motorway.

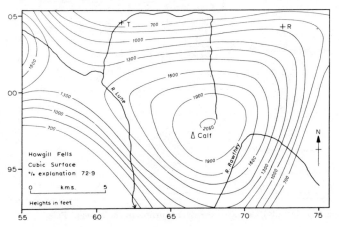

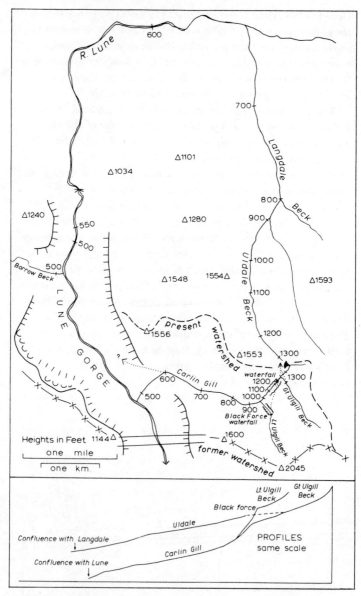

Fig. 2.3 Details of some of the river captures in the Howgill Fells.

Several minor changes of drainage have taken place subsequently in the headwaters of the Lune as a result of the greater
efficiency of the south-flowing streams. This is due to the operation of the law of unequal slopes and to the fact that the Lune
has an important knick-point situated just south of Tebay
[613028]. Some of these captures have been assisted by the
formation of corroms, which are alluvial fans built up in the main
valley by a tributary when the main valley has been left dry by
capture. The fan becomes a corrom when it has built up to a level
that allows water to flow down either its original course or into
the capturing stream's drainage. The streams at the head of Uldale illustrate this process very clearly (see fig. 2.3).

The law of unequal slopes has also operated in favour of the
west-flowing streams against the Ure, which flows east to the
Humber. Thus the Eden has captured the highest headstreams of
the Ure near Hellgill, and the Clough, a tributary of the Lune, has
captured still more of the former Ure drainage, leaving a dry col
on the main watershed at the head of Garsdale [795926]. The
upper five miles of the Ure is now being attacked at separate
points by the Eden and Lune drainage, and will eventually be
diverted to the west (see fig. 2.2). Further disturbance to the
drainage pattern has been caused by glacial interference, but
these effects will be mentioned later.

North of the Howgill Fells the original drainage, as reconstructed by Hollingworth, probably consisted of a series of
streams flowing at right angles to the present Carboniferous
limestone scarp and the Penrith sandstone scarp to join the trunk
stream of the Eden. The dip of the rocks forming the scarps
probably indicates the amount of the Tertiary warping and it was
probably on these rocks, or those of later date that originally
covered them, that the drainage was initiated, as shown in fig.
2.4. As in the areas already mentioned the disruption has been
due to subsequent development in the weaker strata and, as the
older rocks have become exposed, the streams have become discordant to the structures in the area of the Lower Palaeozoic outcrop.

The river Lowther provides a good example of the process of
drainage development in this area. Part of the present Lowther,

from about 5 km north of Shap, consists of a strike stream working back along the base of the Carboniferous scarp and capturing
a series of the original dip streams that flowed at right angles to
the present scarp. The Shap Fell col was probably formed as a
result of the later capture of one of these streams by the Birk
Beck tributary of the Lune. These captures probably did not take
place in an orderly sequence from north to south, but in several
stages. The Whale gap [523215], north of Shap, was most likely
the last to be abandoned as it is one of the deepest. Thus in all
these areas, subsequent stream development along the strike of
the weak rocks as these became exposed, and the operation of
the law of unequal slopes, due to asymmetrical uplift, have been
the main processes by which stream captures and drainage adjust-
ments have taken place (Hollingworth 1929).

The Cheviot Hills In the Cheviot area also, similar forces have
been operating, and Common (1954) suggests that the radial
pattern, associated with the outcrop of the igneous rocks,
developed as a result of modification of an original north-flowing
pattern on the northern flanks of the high ground. The greater
resistance of the igneous rocks led to unequal rates of headward
recession and the preservation of this area as high ground. The
radial pattern is best developed at the eastern end of the massif.
Greater adjustment of structure is evident in the lower reaches of
the rivers, related to the later stages of landscape development. It
is considered that there was initially a watershed between the
high ground 316 m, [081253] east of Chillingham, linking this
hill to the igneous massif (see fig. 4.9). This watershed was
breached by a north-flowing stream and the Hetton and Breamish
streams were diverted to flow north as a result, leaving a dry gap
at Eglingham [105195] to mark their former course. Further
south the river Aln was diverted to the south by a dip-slope tributary of the Coquet near Hulne [160155]. As in all the area there
has been much modification both in detail and, in some instances,
major diversions have occurred as a result of the glacial period,
but these changes will be noted later.

The Lancashire Plain The drainage pattern of the Lancashire

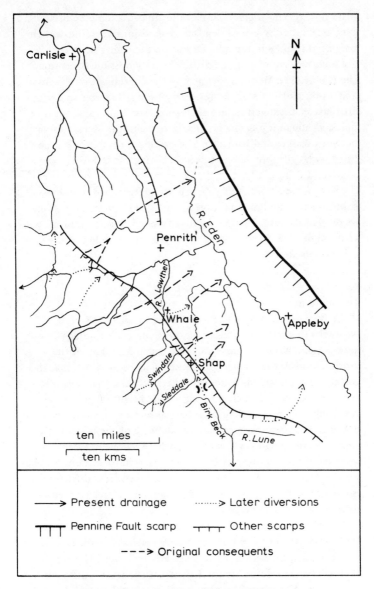

Fig. 2.4 Drainage changes between the Lake District and the river Eden.
(Based on the work of S.E. Hollingworth.)

plain is of recent origin, owing to the almost complete burial of preglacial relief by glacial deposits. The major rivers follow their preglacial courses in the uplands but on the plain they have adopted new courses on the drift. The only possible exception is the Ribble. The Mersey is formed by the confluence of the Goyt and Tame south of Manchester. Part of the river's course is artificial as it is diverted into the Manchester Ship canal for four miles, although it joins its original outlet into the Mersey estuary between Widnes and Runcorn. The preglacial river course is now filled with drift, but can be traced in borings. It follows a course somewhat different from that of the present river. The course of the river Wyre across the Fylde is partly determined by the distribution of drumlins, and it probably differs significantly from its preglacial route. Further details of the postglacial drainage pattern can best be deferred until the character and relief of the drift is considered.

Denudation

Erosion surfaces have been studied in various parts of Northern England by different workers, but their findings do not always agree. Some propose a marine origin for many of the erosion levels, others suggest that the evidence indicates that the surfaces are unwarped, while yet others consider that only a few surfaces are present, each covering a wide height range and representing a warped undulating subaerial surface. In some areas the evidence has been taken to indicate stability of the land in relation to a falling base-level, while elsewhere relatively recent warping of the land surface has been suggested to account for the present landscape. With all these different views it is difficult to correlate the findings of geomorphologists who have worked in different parts of the region.

In order to attempt to arrive at some conclusions concerning the denudation of the whole region the results of work carried out in some areas within it will be briefly reviewed. The areas that will be considered are the Lake District and Howgill Fells, the Forest of Bowland the Alston and Askrigg blocks, the Cheviots and the Isle of Man.

The Lake District and Howgill Fells The denudation chronology of parts of the Lake District has been studied by Hollingworth (1936), McConnell (1938) and Parry (1960b). The former, dealing with the Cumberland and Furness part of the Lake District, suggested, as a result of the study of projected profiles and field evidence, that there was evidence of unwarped horizontal surfaces in the Lake District. The field work established that the surfaces were cut across rocks of different type so that the surfaces in this instance are true erosion surfaces and are not structurally controlled. The higher surfaces are the older, and it is suggested that the relics show evidence of both subaerial and marine erosion. Hollingworth concluded that the unwarped surfaces that he recognised were Mio-Pliocene in age and they occurred at the following levels:

2,550-2,650 ft	780-810 m
2,000-2,100/2,300 ft	610-640/700 m
1,600-1,700 ft	490-520 m
1,000-1,150 ft	300-350 m
700- 800 ft	210-240 m (marine)
570 ft	170 m
400 ft	120 m

The 120 m, 240 m and 300 m surfaces are the most persistent and best developed.

These levels may be compared with those suggested by McConnell for the southeastern part of the Lake District. McConnell thought that the surfaces he recognised were of subaerial origin, and he recorded six levels, with the uppermost being divisible into two parts, thus the total sequence that he gives is as follows:

	Lake District		Howgill Fells	
Ia & b	2,300-2,800 ft	700-850 m	2,000 feet plus	610 m
II	2,000-2,100 ft	610-640 m	1,700-1,850 ft	520-560 m
III	1,500-1,600 ft	460-490 m	1,500-1,600 ft	460-490 m
IV	1,450 ft	440 m	1,250-1,400 ft	380-430 m
V	700-900 (1,150) ft	210-270 m (350)	1,000-1,150 ft	300-350 m
VI	400-450 ft	120-140 m	700- 900 ft	210-270 m

These levels may be compared with a subsequent study by the same author of the Howgill Fells (1939) in which he traced the same surfaces into the Howgill Fells, giving the height ranges for the remnants of subaerial erosion surfaces in this area as shown in the table above. It is apparent that the upper part of the sequence is higher in the Lake District, which he interpreted as due to a greater subsequent uplift of the central Lake District area. The large differences in the lower part of the sequence are not easy to explain but they appear to be due to the grouping of two surfaces together in the Lake District that have been separated in the Howgill Fells. The 460-490 m surface in the Howgill Fells is the best developed and is indicated by flat summits and spur flats.

In many instances the evidence for the lower surfaces is in the form of valley heads and steps, many of which have been affected by glaciation, so that their validity is doubtful. North of the Howgill Fells the abandoned Sunbiggin Tarn valley is the most important remnant of the 210-270 m level. This enables the denudation chronology to be related to the stages of the drainage development.

A more recent study of the erosion of the southeastern Lake District is the work of Parry (1960). His analysis was based on field mapping, and he came to the conclusion that there was evidence for a considerable number of former erosion phases related to higher base levels. He considered that the following levels were represented:

1,300-1,500 ft	400-460 m	(subaerial)
1,000-1,300 ft	300-400 m	(subaerial)
700-800 ft	210-270 m	(subaerial)
690 ft	210 m	(marine)
570 ft	170 m	(marine)
480 ft	150 m	(marine)
430 ft	130 m	(marine)
380 ft	120 m	(marine)
330 ft	100 m	(marine)
290 ft	90 m	(marine)

The upper subaerial surfaces are the oldest and were formed as a result of a falling base-level causing rejuvenation of a subaerial landscape. The lowest subaerial surface is the most widespread.

Parry considers that the subaerial development of the landscape was halted by a slight marine transgression; this initiated the marine sequence of steps. The highest of the marine levels at 210 m is differentiated from the higher subaerial surfaces by the constant level of the break of slope at its rear. It occurs mainly as a valley side bench and does not reach any great width. It occurs on the margins of the foothills of the Lake District. This surface must have been cut when sea-level was at about 200-210 m and the lower surfaces were formed during still stands in a generally falling sea-level. The surfaces are thought to be unwarped and to cut across faults that may date from the Miocene. Thus again a Mio-Pliocene age is suggested for the upper subaerial surfaces. The marine surfaces are considered to be Pleistocene in age by correlation with surfaces of similar origin and elevation elsewhere in Britain.

The evidence as a whole suggests that this part of Northern England has developed under a generally falling base-level during the late Tertiary and Pleistocene period, during which partial erosion surfaces and coastal marine features were formed. The different elevation of the higher surfaces in different parts of the area suggests that differential uplift has taken place during late Tertiary time at least.

The Forest of Bowland The erosion surfaces of the Forest of Bowland have been studied by Moseley (1961) both in the field and by detailed analyses from maps. This area shows both structural control and the effect of erosional processes in the landscape. Evidence of polycyclic landscape development has been found in relics of two main erosion surfaces. These surfaces are thought to be subaerial in origin and owe their characteristics in part to the rock type and structure, as they are preserved on the more resistant rock bands, the structure of which is apparent in the landscape in places. The features in the field that were most useful in differentiating the surfaces were the convex and concave breaks of slope at the lower end upper edges of the surfaces respectively, the slope of the surface itself being at a fairly uniform gradient. The cartographic work included a detailed analysis of the slopes from 1:10,560 maps.

The uppermost surface has been called the Bowland surface and ranges in height from 370 to 520 m. It formed an undulating landscape before the valleys of the Upper Wyresdale surface, at 130 to 300 m were incised into it. This lower surface has itself been dissected by later lowering of base level.

The Bowland surface shows up conspicuously on both field and cartographic surveys. Throughout the height range given above flat areas occur, these are generally the result of the outcrop of gently dipping or horizontal beds of sandstone. The most common elevation of the lower boundary of this surface is a convex break of slope at about 400 m. The base level during the formation of the Bowland surface was probably about or a little below 370 m O.D. The Upper Wyresdale surface rises from 130 m in the west to over 300 m in the east. Its limits are marked by concave breaks of slope above the convex ones below throughout its height range. The majority of flats are related to sandstone bedding planes and the surface has a valley-in-valley form within the upper one. It was created by subaerial erosion related to a base level at about 120-150 m. It is possible that at its lowest level part of this surface is of marine origin, given the well developed concave breaks of slope at its back. The surface has been dissected by the Lower Wyresdale surface which was related to a base level at about 60 m. The two lower levels probably date from the Pliocene, according to Moseley, but a Pleistocene date appears more likely.

Lancashire Plain The Lancashire plain abuts against the Forest of Bowland in the Fylde, but there is little or no evidence of erosion surfaces in this area, which is entirely formed of glacial drift above sea-level. In the southern part of the Lancashire plain, however, there is some evidence of former stages of denudation, as suggested by R.K. Gresswell (1953 and 1964). The surfaces must have been formed after the faulting that has already been mentioned. The sharp relief which would have resulted from these dislocations was reduced to negligible proportions as erosion continued during and after the earth movements. It seems likely that the ice advanced over a surface of low relief. Nevertheless some planation surfaces can be recognised. The three hills on Carboniferous strata already named all reach to a bit over 150 m. These three summits, some of which are ridges, link up with a shelf at the same altitude on the western side of the Forest of Bowland, between Preston and Lancaster, and also with surfaces of similar height in North Wales. This is the highest planation surface in the Lancashire plain.

A profile drawn from Up Holland [520050], between Billinge Hill and Ashurst's Hill towards Ormskirk at Clieves Hill [385080] runs along the crest of a flat-topped ridge. This represents the largest extent of the lower of the two planation surfaces that Gresswell has recognised in this area. It lies at between 60 and 75 m and the higher hills rise fairly sharply above it. The ridge, called the Skelmersdale platform, is 10 km long from west to east and 1.6 km wide. The dominant height is 67 m. It is bordered both at the upper limit and the lower limit by relatively steep slopes, which Gresswell interprets as fossil cliffs. The lower cliff line can be seen at Ormskirk [413085], Clieves Hills [384074], and Aughton [388058]. The surface also occurs in Liverpool at Everton [355920] and Edge Hills [365900]. Other areas representative of the surface are at Olive Mount [390900], Childwall [410890], Mossley Hill [385872], Allerton [413866] and Woolton Park [419873]. It occurs in Wirral, for example at Arno Hill [305873], Bidston [287894], Caldy [222855] and as a wide shelf at Irby [255845], above which there is a fossil cliff leading up to Thurstaston Hill. There is some evidence of a rather lower surface at about 47 m, for example in Liverpool at [358905]. Gresswell is of the opinion that these surfaces represent preglacial abrasion platforms, and he would thus support a marine origin. In view of their coastal situation this seems a reasonable assumption and their relatively small size would not preclude this possibility.

The Alston and Askrigg blocks The forms of a land surface can be assessed by means of trend surface analysis. This technique has been applied to the summit erosion surface of the Askrigg and Alston blocks (King 1969). The summit surface was defined by summit spot heights derived from O.S. maps. The quadratic surface for the Alston block accounts for 89% of the total sums of squares, while the cubic surface for the Askrigg blocks accounts

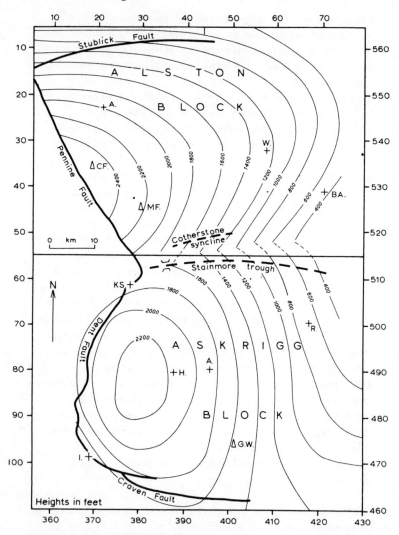

Fig. 2.5 Trend surface of the central Pennines. A quadratic surface has been fitted to the *a)* Alston block summit heights and cubic surface to those of the Askrigg block. They meet in a trough close to the Stainmore depression. *Opposite b)* Structure contours on the base of the Main (Great) Limestone are shown relative to O.D. in feet. (After Dunham 1974.)

for 78.5%. The two surfaces are shown linked in figure 2.5. The
link between the surfaces forms an eastward sloping trough,
which closely approximates to the position of the Stainmore syncline. Structural elements are reflected in the trend of the surface,
which appears to give a good indication of the nature of the
warping of the erosion surface that was uplifted in the late Tertiary period (see fig. 2.5b).

The structure contours run nearly parallel to the trend surface
contours over much of the area, while the Carboniferous structure itself reflects the control of the underlying basement, in

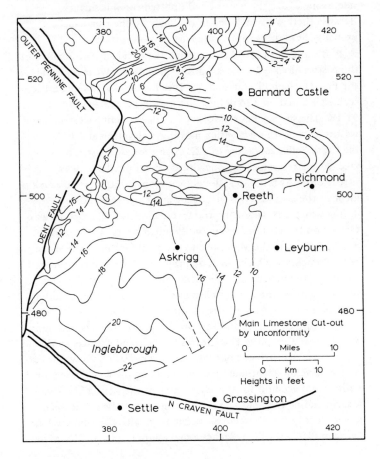

which the Weardale and Wensleydale granite masses are particularly important. The Teesdale anticline and the Stainmore trough are both closely reflected in the trend surface. These structures appear to affect the drainage pattern, the streams flowing at right angles to the trend surface contours over much of the area.

The pattern of residuals supports the suggestion that some of the major valleys, including Wensleydale, may have been initiated along minor downwarps in the uplifted surface as they lie along belts of negative anomalies. The positive residuals represent monadnocks, including Cross Fell, Mickle Fell and Great Whernside, rising above the warped and uplifted summit surface. Because there were included in the analysis, the trend surface probably lies fairly close to the true erosion surface.

P. Beaumont (1970) has extended the trend surface analysis of the Alston block 32 km eastward to include the Wear Lowlands, the East Durham Plateau and the Tees Lowlands. The quadratic surface is based on 326 points, and it gives an explanation of 91.1%. The surface has the form of a ridge trending west-south-west to east-north-east, with a maximum elevation at 790 m in the Cross Fell area, falling to 122 m on the east coast. This surface closely resembles the one already mentioned that was fitted to the Alston block alone. Beaumont interprets the development of the area in terms of Eocene and Oligocene erosion, during which any Mesozoic strata were eroded and a surface was formed on the Carboniferous and Permian strata. This surface was domed up in the Miocene and marginal faulting created the Alston block, on which radial drainage developed on the tilted surface of the peneplain. Subsequent development of the stream system initiated the present elements of the landscape, including the East Durham Plateau. The rigidity of the Alston block is due to the Weardale granite and the low density of rock also account for the isostatic uplift. The streams fit the trend surface, so that the peneplaned surface must have been very flat to allow this pattern to develop. Continued movement along the western marginal faults could account for the asymmetry of the Alston block valleys, including the South Tyne, East and West Allen. The Proto-lower Wear became a major subsequent stream, isolating the East Durham Plateau, which reaches a maximum height of 218 m, but is elsewhere at 150 m to 180 m. Still lower surfaces have been formed in the Wear Lowland area at elevations of 98 m, 58 m, 43 m and 30 m. The lower of the surfaces are probably post-glacial in date, being related to changes in the Wear drainage pattern resulting from the glacial diversions.

In the Askrigg block structural control must be carefully considered in elucidating the denudation chronology. In the south the Craven Highlands consist of large areas of limestone outcrop, much of which has been studied by Sweeting (1950) and Waltham (1971). There is evidence in this area for a widespread erosion surface at about 450 m. Sweeting has shown that it is a true erosion surface as, although it extends widely over the limestone, it has also been traced onto other rock types. It may correlate with the Bowland surface to the south. If this is so, then, as Moseley has pointed out, its formation must post-date movement along the Craven faults.

The Wyresdale surface may also correlate with the Dales stage described by Sweeting. This later stage in the development of the Craven Highlands is indicated by rejuvenation in the major dales, indicating a former base-level at about 290 m.

A later stage of development is also suggested by a second and lower rejuvenation head. This lower stage is probably responsible for the major knick-points in the streams of the Askrigg block. There are conspicuous waterfalls where the knick-points have been held up by hard rocks, for example the Aysgarth Falls [020890] in Wensleydale. Knick-points corresponding to that in the Ure near Aysgarth are conspicuous in many of the major rivers. The Lune has a marked knick-point just south of Tebay and the North Tyne also has one. Its profile has been studied by Peel (1941), who suggests by mathematical extrapolation that the base-level before the initiation of the knick-point was at 50 m. Terrace evidence supports this height estimation, which on its own is of doubtful validity.

North of the main limestone outcrop in the Askrigg block structural control of the landscape is the dominant characteristic. The almost flat-lying, resistant bands of limestone, sandstone and Millstone Grit, the latter often capping the higher hill tops, give rise to areas of flat land, with the shale outcropping on the

steeper slopes between. The whole landscape slopes gently eastwards with the gentle dip of the strata in this direction. The surface slopes east at from ½ degree in the west to about 1 degree in
the east. This is a gentler gradient than the dip of the rocks, so
that the newer rocks outcrop eastwards. This suggests, and the
trend surface analysis supports the view, that the surface is a
warped peneplain, uplifted at the end of the Tertiary era. The
same type of evolution has already been suggested for the adjacent Alston block to the north, where a peneplain also appears to
have been warped and uplifted at this time.

G. de Boer (1974) has considered the physiographic evolution
of Yorkshire. The dating of the Cleveland dyke to at least 58
million years ago, in the Lower Eocene (?), gives longer for the
geomorphological development, and makes an early Tertiary
peneplain a possibility. The contrast between stable shelves and
subsiding gulfs and basins, supported by the geophysical data, is
significant, and gives rise to the geomorphological contrasts. A
mainly subaerial, polycyclic development seems most likely. Uplift relatively late in the Tertiary, possibly in the Pliocene, seems
reasonable. The Askrigg block surface slopes east at 25 m / km
from Great Whernside eastwards, possibly representing a stripped
sub-Permian surface, as the slope is similar to that of the base of
the Permian. Westwards, ridges rise to a height 90 to 150 m
higher, forming a plateau, which meets the ramp at 550 m around
Penhill in Wensleydale, running from [NZ 0007] at Faggerhill
Moor to Meugher [SE 044705]. The plateau is probably a dissected peneplain with monadnocks, rising to 610 m where it crosses
the Dent Fault.

Two major stages led first to a 400 m surface, sloping from
425 to 380 m, and second to a further valley incision to 120 to
150 m below the higher surface. All the major streams have knick
points at the limit of a still later incision, for example in Leck
Beck at [SD 659799] and the Wharfe at [SD 991646]. North of
the Great Scar limestone outcrop structural benches make surface
recognition difficult. The relationship of the Askrigg and Alston
blocks peneplain with the Howgill Fells summit surface is difficult. The Calf could be a monadnock, as is Great Whernside, so
that the Pennine peneplain would be equivalent to the second

surface of the Howgill Fells, not the highest one. If the Chalk cover was thin over the Pennines, there can only have been limited erosion of the upper peneplain surface. Drainage on the Askrigg block is radial from Widdale Fell, and results from (a) eastward tilting, (b) effects of uplift and warping of the peneplain, and (c) adjustment to structure, the events possibly taking place in this order. The Swale and Ure lie in a general downwarp, between an anticlinal area to the north of the Swale and the half dome to the south. The Swale has its longest tributaries from the north and the Ure from the south. These two main rivers were the original easterly consequents and uplift and warping created the south and west flowing streams, completing the radial pattern.

The Cheviot Hills Common's work (1954) in the east Cheviots area shows that remnants of erosion surfaces can be traced, particularly on the igneous outcrop where alone the upper surfaces occur. The following main levels are thought to be of major importance. A surface at 290 m to 300-370 m has fairly extensive remnants mainly on the ridges, another lower one from 230-170 m to 150 m is also found on the ridges. Remnants at 400 to 460 m occur mainly in the southwest. There are also surfaces above this height at 470 m to 490 m to 520 m on the watershed and accordant summits at 530 to 560 m occur at the highest levels. These upper levels are less well marked than the first three mentioned. These features, cut into the igneous rocks, are true erosion surfaces, but on the sedimentary rocks around, some of the features are structurally controlled.

The Isle of Man The southern part of the Isle of Man shows clearly the Caledonian trend in its two major mountain ridges, running approximately northeast to southwest. These mountains end abruptly to the north along an east-west line. This may represent a modified cliff line as the old rocks continue to the north and the subdrift surface appears to be a buried marine abrasion surface falling slowly to the north and then dropping off more rapidly just south of the Point of Ayre (see section EF, fig. 2.6). The landscape gives evidence of fairly recent and asymmetrical uplift. The hill summits rise gently from an upland surface of gently rolling moorland, covering a height range from about 230 to 370 m. This may well be analogous to the Bowland surface already described, although at a lower elevation owing to less uplift, but similarly representing a rolling subaerial surface that has subsequently been uplifted and dissected.

This later dissection is particularly clearly seen in the north, where the rolling upland surface is deeply dissected by steep

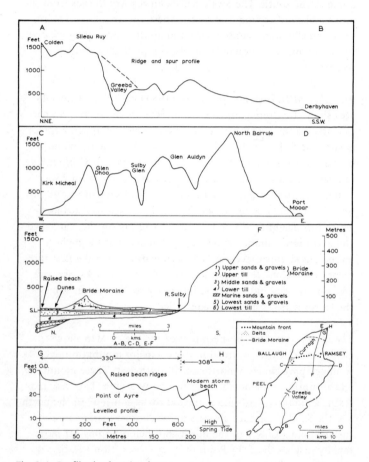

Fig. 2.6 Profiles in the Isle of Man.

north-flowing streams, of which Sulby Glen is the largest, (see profile CD fig. 2.6). The steep gradient of these streams, draining the steep northern face of the mountain group, helps to account for the greater dissection of the upland surface in this part of the island. When viewed from the south coast the mountain area appears to rise up in a series of steps, suggesting that uplift has taken place in stages, (see section AB, fig. 2.6 and fig. 2.7). A level around 150 to 180 m is especially conspicuous in the centre

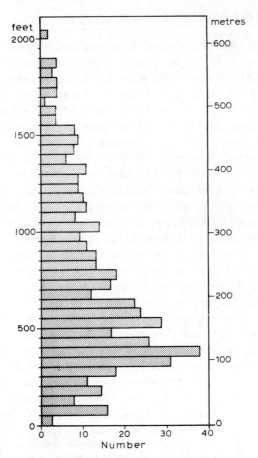

Fig. 2.7 Altimetric analysis of the Isle of Man suggesting erosion surfaces.

of the island and can also be traced around the coast in other
parts such as around Dreemskerry [473913] in the east. There is
a surface at 150 to 180 m into which Glen Roy is incised west of
Laxey [435840], and a broad surface at about this elevation
occurs west of Douglas and in the extreme southwest near Port
Erin and Port St Mary. A coastal plain at about 90 m occurs
south of Peel and along the coastal strip between Castletown and
Douglas, although it is modified by glacial deposits in places.

General conclusions concerning denudation
One of the major problems of landscape development in
Northern England is to reconcile the view that the upland landscape consists of a single warped and uplifted peneplain, as
suggested by Trotter for the Alston block, and the evidence produced in other parts for the formation of many erosion surfaces
related to different base-levels. The variety of levels suggested for
different areas is summarised diagrammatically in fig. 2.8. As
Moseley states it is difficult to imagine a base level almost 370 m
above the present during the Tertiary, thus there is something to
recommend the view that the landscape is the result of the warping and uplifting of one surface during the late Tertiary to early
Pleistocene period with the subsequent erosion taking place in
stages during the Pleistocene. The youthful stage of development
of the landscape on the Alston block is strong evidence for the
late date of the uplift of this surface, although it is possible that
uplift took place here at a more recent date than elsewhere in the
region. If this were so, then the changes in base level seem to be
more reasonably explained by movement of the land as well as
the sea, and purely eustatic control of base level is less likely.
Under these conditions correlation by altitude would not be expected, at least for the earlier and higher surfaces, while the lower
ones, such as the ones below 300 m could be related to a later
period of Pleistocene date, when relative stability had been
reached within the area. The lack of correlation by altitude between the Howgill Fells and central Lake District at the upper
levels supports the view that differential land uplift, rather than a
fall of sea-level, is responsible for the erosion surface development.

Offshore subsidence accompanying land upheaval would help

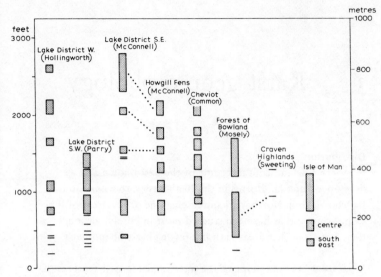

Fig. 2.8 Diagram to illustrate the different erosion levels suggested by various geomorphologists for parts of Northern England.

to account for the rejuvenation that is so characteristic of the area. The gravity survey of Bott (1964) supports the view that basin subsidence has been in progress for a long time in the Irish Sea on either side of the ridge of older rocks connecting the Isle of Man to the Lake District. Such a tendency could well be balanced by local uplift over the land areas. Such subsidence could have separated the Isle of Man from the Lake District, with which it is most closely associated geologically.

3   Karst geomorphology

Distribution

Northern England contains some of the best-known and well developed karst landforms in the British Isles, the area around Ingleborough in North Yorkshire being one of the areas of limestone scenery that has been studied most intensely, although there are also other areas with interesting karst phenomena.

Northwest Yorkshire One of the most characteristic features of the Craven Uplands is the development of karst features on the extensive limestone outcrop. Some of these features are shown in fig. 3.1a. The area contains both surface and subterranean phenomena of great interest and variety. One of the early works on this area by M.M. Sweeting (1950) related the systems of cave passages and pitches, the former being essentially horizontal and the latter vertical, to the stages of landscape development. The passages were thought to have developed during a relative still-stand of base level, when an erosion surface was forming, and the water table was fairly stable. The pitches, on the other hand, were thought to have formed during stages of rejuvenation, when the base level was falling and incision allowed the water table to fall also. Thus underground evidence was suggested to support the proposed denudation chronology. More recent work has modified this theory, as will be discussed when the subterranean features are considered.

The landforms of the limestone areas of Northern England are influenced by three major variables, according to Sweeting (1974), the lithology, the tectonics and Pleistocene glaciation, and it is the variations of these three variables that cause the distinctive limestone landforms of different parts of the area. The largest limestone outcrop occurs in the Igleborough-Malham area where the little disturbed strata of the Great Scar limestone outcrop over a wide area. This area has also been considerably influenced by the more recent Pleistocene ice advances, in contrast to the limestone areas of the southern Peak District and the Mendip Hills.

The Morecambe Bay area Limestone outcrops widely in the Carboniferous scarp south of the Lake District around Morecambe Bay. This limestone area extends from Kirkby Lonsdale to the north shore of Morecambe Bay and Furness (fig. 3.1b). The limestones include thick micrites, sparites and pseudobreccias. These strata vary laterally and lack reefs. They are divided by faults into northsouth blocks, and dip eastwards, with westerly downthrows, giving a step-like structure and relief. The dips vary from block to block and are mainly steeper than in the Craven district. The limestones were deposited on a flatter surface than those in the Ingleborough area, and they now outcrop at heights between 100 and 300 m O.D. They have been exposed since the Permo-Triassic period, while the limestones of the Ingleborough area have only been exposed since the Pleistocene. An early phase of karstification in the Morecambe Bay area occurred before the deposition of the Trias. It has been modified by a period of warm climate in the Tertiary and by the cold conditions of the Pleistocene, when it was scoured by moving ice, and drift was deposited in places. Many of the caves of this area have been eroded away. One view considers that the limestone represents relics of tropical karst conditions, because the limestone forms high ground, and this rock is resistant under tropical conditions, but this is only one possible explanation.

The limestone is very broken into separate blocks, thus hollows are not common. There are some dolines, however, for example near Yealand Redmayne [500760] and Beetham [500800], where they are 400 m across and have flat floors of planed limestone. The area is essentially one of glaciated karst, with many bare surfaces and perched blocks. Dips are mainly between 10 and 25 degrees, and glacial scour has produced bare dip slopes and steep cliffs, as on Hutton Roof Crag [580780] and

Hampsfell, near Grange [410780]. Grikes, runnels and grooves have developed, and they are long due to the inclined surfaces, reaching a length of 15 m. The runnels are Rundkarren, but some sharp *Rinnenkarren*, formed by free air solution, also occur. The

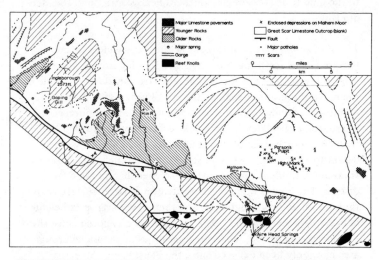

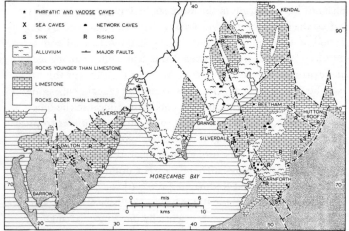

Fig. 3.1 *Top a)* Some karstic features of the area around Ingleborough and Malham. *Above b)* Some karstic features of the area around Morecambe Bay.

rounded type form under vegetation. The less massively bedded limestones have been much affected by frost, for example at Arnside Knott [456775] and Helsington Burrows [490905] near Kendal. Stratified screes are abundant and suggest climatic change. They occur, for example, on Arnside Knott [456775] and Whitbarrow Scar [440870] and indicate severe cold and effective frost action during some phases.

Northeast of the Lake District There are also outcrops of limestone around the northeastern fringe of the Lake District Carboniferous outcrop. One small area of well developed limestone pavement occurs along the line of the Dent fault near Ravenstonedale. The outcrop, known as The Clouds [740000] is in the form of a southerly pitching anticline. The limestone is highly jointed and a complex pavement, with well developed grikes follows the structures closely, with small inward facing scars around the curved pavement. Other pavements occur north of Ravenstonedale, where the limestone again outcrops between Crosby Garrett and Orton. The pavements are small and the limestone intensely weathered, as the bedding is thin. The area has been ice-covered at times, as Shap granite erratics occur on the limestone. The pavement, for example at [687093] west of Crosby Garrett, is very rough surfaced and broken compared to those of the Ingleborough area.

Geological controls
The geological controls affecting the karst features of Northern England include the occurrence of shale bands, the lithology of the limestone, the structure, the joint pattern and the effect of faults. Moisley (1953-4) has suggested that the pavements formed where paper-thin shale bands held up percolating waters for long enough to enhance the solution along bedding planes in the limestone, where it lies almost horizontally over the Ingleborough-Malham area. The pavements are well developed in this area, where they are characterised by clints and grikes.

The lithology varies from fine porcellaneous beds to sparry limestone, with 90% sparry calcite. The major variations are vertical rather than horizontal. The type of lithology affects the character of the scars, through their different reaction to weathering and erosion. The sparry limestones are more massive than the biomicrites and micrites, such as the Porcellaneous Bed. The weak shale bands are also important. The sparry limestones have a lower porosity of 2-3%, and are less soluble than the biomicrites, which have a porosity of 8%.

The affects of structure and tectonics in the Ingleborough-Malham area are related to the high elevation of the limestone above the surrounding lowlands. The karst area is thus free-draining and uplift is still taking place among the bounding faults of the Askrigg block; tremors occurred for example in 1947 and 1970. The recent and considerable uplift is partly responsible for the common occurrence of vertical potholes and shafts, especially in the south of the area. Tertiary erosion is based on warping and uplift of the erosion surface, which has been revealed by trend surface analysis, and this helps to explain both the drainage development and the karst features. The highest point of the surface is near Capon Hall [867667], south of Fountains Fell [870705] at 460 m where the level of the pre-Carboniferous floor is at 460 m. There is a structural high from Fountains Fell to Malham Moor. This pattern could explain the turning of the lines of springs from west to east to north to south in the upper Ribble and upper Wharfe valleys. The pattern of curving valleys is basically structural, but has been modified to form through valleys by glacial erosion, as confirmed by the trend surface analysis (Sweeting 1974).

The most mature karst is in the high level Fountains Fell-Dodd Fell [840845] axis, where the limestone is highest. The pre-Carboniferous floor is over 360 m around Malham Tarn, but it is only at 240 m near Ingleton. The regional dip is north and must initially have·been steeper, and the strata have since been tilted back to their present position, as indicated by the warping of the summit erosion surface. In its early history of erosion the surface sloped south. Thus all the streams on the south side of the block drain south. There may be some relict valleys of an earlier north-south system, such as that between Knowe Fell [870687] and Highfolds Ridge behind Tarn House [893672], or that leading to Middle House [907681]. The whole area may be described as a

Randebene (karst margin plain), a typical karst landform. The
planed area truncates the lower limestone beds and the pre-
Carboniferous rocks. Structural and associated erosional processes are thus important in accounting for the karst features,
especially the major landforms and state of development.

The details of the limestone features depend markedly on
joint frequency. There may well be a close relationship between
joint frequency and the incidence of limestone pavements.
Sweeting (1966) points out that in the more massive beds vertical
joints predominate, while horizontal bedding planes form the
dominant lines of weakness in the thinly bedded layers. Doughty
(1968) has studied the formation of limestone scars in relation to
joint frequency. He has established nine units in the Great Scar
limestone of the Ingleborough district in which joint density
decreased from a high frequency at the base of the unit to low
values at the top. The higher joint frequency was associated with
carbonate sandstone at the base, and the lower with carbonate
mudstone at the top of the unit. He suggests that the closely
spaced joints allow water to penetrate more readily and then it is
held up at the less closely jointed horizons at the top of the next
unit, allowing solution to be concentrated at this point. This
view avoids the necessity for shale bands, for which there is sometimes no evidence.

Geomorphological controls
The most important geomorphological controls to be mentioned
are the controls on solution of the limestone, and the effects of
glaciation. Solution is the most effective agent in removing limestone. The Norber boulder pedestals [768700] give some indication of the importance of solution in lowering the surface.
Recent quantitative observations of the amount of carbonate in
karst waters have indicated a rate of lowering of the surface of
0.04 mm/year, while 0.043 mm/year is lost by underground
solution. The values agree well with the evidence of the perched
blocks. Locally solution can be very rapid where acid peaty
waters, for instance, drain directly onto the limestone. Runnels
7 to 15 cm deep were cut in thirteen years under these conditions
(Sweeting 1966).

The effects of glaciation have been interpreted differently by various workers. Parry (1960) considers that the pavements retreat along strike lines by collapse. He is of the opinion that the Main Dales glaciation was too long ago to account for the present form of the pavements, and suggests that they may have formed by snow bank solution up to about 7500 B.C. in zone IV. Snow can hold more carbon dioxide than water and hence cause more solution of limestone. He considers that this process could operate effectively on the reversed slopes of the pavements, and that in warmer conditions, as at present, the pavements are tending to be buried under debris and decay.

It seems likely that the most important agent causing the stripping of the surface soil and vegetation to reveal the scars and pavements so characteristic of the Craven karst area was achieved by the erosion of the glaciers that overran the area in the later stages of the Devensian, culminating about 15,000 to 20,000 years ago. Kilnsey Crags [974682] show particularly clearly the effects of glacial scour and rounding, in the well developed overhang. Where the rock is thinly bedded the scars have subsequently been reduced to small dimensions by scree formation at their foot. Frost action is the most effective agent in causing block falls and creating scree, but it is acting more slowly at present than in the colder phases of the late and postglacial periods, when the area was under periglacial conditions.

Glacial meltwater played a large part in enlarging the limestone passages towards the end of the glacial period, and rejuvenation has also affected the drainage, creating gorges, knickpoints and waterfalls. Meltwaters have deepened some valleys also, such as Leck Beck valley [650780] and Trow Gill [757717]. Till of recent date is widespread, and there is evidence of considerable glacial erosion. Overdeepening by 60 m has taken place in Wharfedale and Littondale. The glacial erosion was most severe on exposed slopes, thus the northern slope of Penyghent has been smoothed by ice action, while drift has been deposited on the sheltered, lee slopes, as on Newby Moss [740720] and Ireby Fell [668767] south of Gragareth. K.M. Clayton (1966) has suggested that limestone pavements appear to form best under a thin drift cover, which keeps the limestone wet. As vegetation is removed the limestone becomes fretted and loses its smoothness. Direct, nearly instantaneous solution by falling rain causes the fretting.

Surface karst features

A variety of surface features are typical of the karst area. These include large features, such as various types of hollows, and smaller features, such as the clints and grikes that develop on the exposed limestone pavements.

Dolines and similar enclosed hollows have developed, and smaller swallow holes, or shake holes as they are called locally, outline the upper edge of the limestone outcrop. Springs indicate the lower limit of the limestone outcrop. The fact that shake holes surround many drumlins on the limestone indicates that the smaller hollows at least are of postglacial origin. The entrance to many large caves and sink holes lies above the boundary between the Yoredale rocks and the Great Scar limestone, but streams mainly sink into small pot holes at the Yoredale or till border. The shale boundary has been pushed back 600 m in places around Ingleborough. Shake holes occur where drift sinks into subsidence cones resulting from solution of the limestone below a thin drift cover. They are numerous where the drift is 2-3 m thick, but rare where it is more than 10 m thick. At times they occur around thick drift, and along buried shale-limestone boundaries.

The larger enclosed hollows, described by Clayton (1966), are the most mature karst features, although they only represent early maturity. The hollows reach 800 m across and up to 100 m deep. They occur mainly on Parson's Pulpit [918687] near Malham Tarn. They are not collapse features, but appear to have formed where solution was concentrated under a thin soil cover in a hollow. The hollow would be enlarged as more moisture drained towards it. As it deepened a limestone scar would be exposed around its margins and this would retreat by recession of the free face. These larger hollows, unlike the small swallow holes, are probably preglacial in origin. The small enclosed swallow holes have formed by surface solution, where water drained off drift or impermeable strata. R.J. Jones (1965) has stressed the importance of vegetation in limestone solution, concluding that most grike and clint formation takes place beneath vegetation, where organic acids are present.

The larger hollows on High Mark [930677] and Parson's Pulpit may, according to Sweeting (1974), represent hollows on the edge of earlier shale outcrops now removed, as large closed hollows tend to develop on the shale-limestone boundary. They remain because debris collects in them, allowing them to remain damp and continue to dissolve by peat and humic acids, providing an instance of positive feedback. They are wide relative to their depth, as opposed to pot holes, which are deep compared to their width. The pot holes have deep, fluted solutional shafts. They occur in strong limestone beds, and are related to stony and sandy till, but not to the shale junction. There are 20 pot holes in one square kilometre on the Allotment of Ingleborough, which is drift covered. These features are related to glaciation and they could have been formed under an ice cap by glacial meltwater, having been widened later by peaty waters.

One of the more striking features of the karst areas of Northern England is the large extent of bare limestone pavements. These features are largely absent in the limestone areas of the southern Peak District and the Mendips, probably because these areas were not affected by the latest glaciation in the Devensian. The pavements consist of flat-topped clints separated by widened joints, called grikes. In sparry limestone the clints are larger, a mean size being 2 m by 1 m, with a maximum of 100 m^2. Biomicrites tend to flake, especially under frost action. Grikes are deep and narrow in sparry limestone, being 0.12 to 0.25 m wide and 2 to 3 m deep, in less sparry limestone they are 0.25 to 1 m wide and 0.5 to 1 m deep. The grikes are of two forms; there are the widened joints and the smaller type, which has a dentritic pattern and which are entirely due to solution by moving water. The covering soil was removed by ice, and at present the surface is sensitive to climatic and cultural change. The vegetation has changed much in the postglacial period and now sheep and cows cause a reduction in the vegetation cover. Pedestals up to 0.30 m high occur under erratics on the more susceptible beds, for example under the Norber boulders [766700]. The pavements are probably relict landforms. The rounded type of grike, called

Rundkarren, were probably initiated by solution due to acid peaty waters and they were most likely formed under vegetation, when it was more widespread; they are often about 0.25 m deep and 1 to 2 m long. The grikes have probably formed since the deposition of the erratics about 12,000 years ago. Little solution goes on under till, but when the pavement becomes exposed, striations are removed by solution in 10 years, and in places 100 mm incision has been recorded between 1951 and 1970 (Sweeting 1974), by streams draining off the till. The sharp *Rillenkarren* are produced by instantaneous solution caused by falling rain water.

The limestone pavements of Craven have been measured in detail by H. Goldie (1973), between Twisleton Scar in the west near Ingleton and the east side of Wharfedale. The size of clint, type of grike and limestone were recorded at 50 sites, at which five samples were recorded in a 10 by 10 m square area. The details of the measurements are as follows:

	Clint length m		Clint width m		Grike depth m		Grike width cm	
	mean	st. dev.	mean	st. dev.	mean	st. dev.	mean	st. dev.
Ingleborough	3.35	3.16	1.47	1.23	1.07	0.49	20.42	10.08
Malham	2.41	2.06	0.89	0.46	0.97	0.46	19.25	13.94
Wharfedale	1.85	0.91	0.91	0.50	0.78	0.28	18.74	13.51

The numbers of observations at each site were 145 at Ingleborough, 35 at Malham and 70 in Wharfedale. The Ingleborough site has the more massive pavements, the Malham site the older ones and the Wharfedale area has been more disturbed by man. The least dissected pavements are Scar Close, Borrins Moor Rocks, Southern Scale, Scales Moor and Malham Cove. The most dissected are White Scars, Raven Scar and Threshfield. On the whole it was found that the largest clints occurred in the centre of traverses across the limestone outcrop, with smaller ones at the inner edge due to more aggressive water and the outer edge due to more effective pressure release. The more massive pavements of the central section are attributed to more effective glacial scouring. The pavements are most massive and best developed where glacial scouring was at a maximum, for the ice cut deeper into the surface to expose massive and little-weathered beds. The distribution of drift is also important, and the type of limestone. Sparry calcite in the limestone tends to be associated with better developed pavements. The orientation measurements agreed on the whole with those made by Wager (1931), and showed no particular bias in relation to wide and deep grikes.

Subterranean karst features

There are very extensive cave systems underground in the karst areas of Northern England. These systems have been explored and much is known of their pattern and origin, although there is still more exploration to be done. Some points concerning the karst hydrology will first be mentioned, followed by an account of the types, development and chronology of the cave systems, and finally some specific cave systems will be briefly described.

Karst hydrology The relationships between dissolved calcium carbonate and the rate of water circulation in the central Pennine springs has been studied by J.L. Ternan (1972). When the calcium carbonate varies rapidly, the passage of allogenic water through open swallets is indicated, and this water moves quickly through the limestone. More uniform calcium carbonate content is associated with slow water movement by diffuse percolation. There is a well integrated water drainage system associated with the first situation. Diffuse percolation refers to the slow recharge through soil water infiltration with lesser conduit development. The temporal variability in water hardness correlates highly with flow-through time. The results were obtained by sampling in the High Mark-Fountains Fell area near Malham Tarn. The High Mark area is at 457 to 538 m and is almost entirely limestone. No surface drainage exists so that all the recharge is by diffuse percolation. On Fountains Fell there is a cap of Yoredale and Millstone Grit strata, allowing allogenic streams to flow onto the limestone, although diffuse percolation also occurs. The mean variability of calcium hardness ($V = \sigma / \overline{X} \times 100$, where σ is the standard deviation and $\overline{X}$ is the mean) is 5.8% in the High Mark springs with a range of variation of 2.2 to 10.6%. On Fountains Fell the mean value is 13.5%. A t-test showed a significant difference at 0.005 confidence level. A seasonal trend exists, reach-

ing a peak in mid-summer to autumn, due to increased bio-
chemical production of carbon dioxide at higher temperatures.
Shorter-term fluctuations are related to rainfall. The flow-through
times were more rapid on Fountains Fell, varying mainly from 4
to 12 days, while on High Mark the times were between 10 and
80 days.

Calcium carbonate, temperature and water volumes have been
recorded at 5 resurgences on Darnbrook Fell [880722] at two
weekly intervals over one year by Ternan (1974). The mean calcium carbonate value was 128 ppm, a fairly low value, similar to
that of the surface waters in the area, because of the high
addition of swallet water. Percolation water enters quickly into
the system and cannot readily be differentiated. The temperature
measurements suggest discrete water flows. Observations by
A.F. Pitty (1974) show that the calcium carbonate in water
descending Gaping Gill is an inverse function of precipitation.
Water moves rapidly to Clapham Beck Head as the 0 to 2 day
relationship between inflow and outflow is important, illustrating
both the cause and effect of a large cave system. In northwest
Yorkshire the water draining onto the Great Scar limestone
already has considerable calcium carbonate content due to the
Yoredale limestones and the resurgences only show a slight increase. The calcium carbonate content is low compared with the
Mendips. This is due to the large volume of water flowing
through the cave systems, reflecting a high ratio of swallet water
to percolation water, at least in the major cave systems, such as
Borrins Moor [765752] to Alum Pot [775755] and Tarn Dub
near Penyghent.

The deposition of tufa in Gordale Beck [915641] has been
studied by Pitty (1971). He collected water samples monthly and
these showed a positive correlation of calcium carbonate with
temperature. Peaks occurred in midsummer and autumn. The
absolute peak was in autumn and is related to the high production of carbon dioxide in summer and the time lag, reflecting
flow-through time. The station below the tufa screen always
recorded lower values, possibly owing to continuous photo-
synthesis throughout the year, resulting from the comparatively
high temperatures. Tufa formation is associated with mosses and

algae, and seasonal variations are related to variations in plant
activity through the year.

The cave systems The cave systems of the Ingleborough district
have been reassessed by A.C. Waltham (1970). He notes the significance of passage morphology in relation to the positions of
the passages in the vadose or phreatic zones. In this area there are
both vadose and phreatic types, the former are generally T-shaped
with a flat roof formed often along a thin shale parting of a bedding plane (see fig. 3.2). The phreatic passages are more circular;
having been eroded by water under pressure they can have
reversed floor gradients. They have various forms of roof solution,
but many are now dry, indicating that they were formed under
different hydrological conditions, before the recent incision
leading to a fall of water level in the bedrock. In preglacial times
vadose channels fed into a phreatic system.

The vadose cave systems are more numerous, and the passages
smaller usually than the preatic ones. The vadose caves show
strong geological control, forming either gently-sloping bedding
plane openings with continuously downhill-sloping floors, or
steep, often vertical passages formed along a joint or fault. The
vertical shafts may be up to 100 m deep. Many of the vadose
systems descend to the present valley floors and are integral parts
of the current drainage pattern. These vadose caves must post-
date the valley floor excavation. They are younger than the
phreatic system. Thus the northwest Yorkshire caves can be
classified into older, preglacial phreatic systems, and younger,
postglacial vadose ones.

The systems are formed in the Great Scar limestone, which is
168 m thick, dipping at 1 to 4 degrees north, with shallow folds.
Joints are mainly vertical, trending northwest-southeast and 0.5
to 3 m apart. There are also minor faults. Shale bands from 0.1 to
2 m thick occur and are concentrated in three main stratigraphic
zones, which determine the pattern of passages with regard to
elevation. The surface is a dissected plateau, which is erosional in
the Malham area and structurally controlled elsewhere, as on
Scales Moor [720770] . The main valleys drain south and were
deepened during the Pleistocene, largely by glaciers. Glaciated

karst features abound, including pavements, low angle scars and shakeholes in the overlying till. Dry valleys formed in three ways; some were formed by fluvial erosion in a cold climate, such as Watlowes, a few others are due to collapse of caves, such as Trow Gill, and a few shallow ones on till have developed recently and been left dry as the water drained through the till. For sizeable caves to form the drainage must be effective and efficient. Before glacial excavation of the valleys, phreatic tubes were formed. The pattern of major tubes developed along the maximum hydraulic gradient towards the lower Craven Lowlands to the southwest, preferring the most soluble limestones or those with other weaknesses, with flow against the regional dip, and with preferential development along the major joints and bedding planes. In postglacial times the system became vadose as water could now pass freely downwards. There is no trace of water-table control on cave development, but structural and stratigraphic controls are

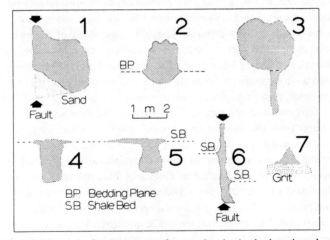

Fig. 3.2 Diagrams of various types of caves, showing both phreatic and vadose types. (After A.C. Waltham.) 1. Large phreatic tube with some glacial fill. 2. phreatic passage along bedding plane, with upper bed more soluble. 3. large phreatic tube with narrow, younger vadose canyon in its floor. 4. vadose canyon incised below bedding plane. 5. vadose canyon incised below very wide shale bed opening. 6. vadose rift passage formed along a fault. 7. essentially vadose passage, wide floor due to resistant grit bed.

important, especially joints, faults, and shale bands. Cave passages are concentrated in the zones where shales abound, and these vary in elevation. Most of the vadose systems flow down dip, northwards, except where modified by local folding or where they invade earlier phreatic passages.

The cave systems are small on the whole, with passages only 0.6 m wide and rarely exceeding 6 m^2 section, the longest passages known are only 5 km long (Waltham 1972). Vadose caves are usually canyon-like and are high and narrow. Large phreatic tubes are about 4.5 m in diameter. Collapse and blockage is common in the abandoned ones. Most vadose passages are active and clean cut, some are decorated. Older decorated passages are mainly phreatic in origin, and occur up to 60 to 100 m above the present valley levels and resurgences.

A.C. Waltham (1974) has pointed out that a chronological division of the cave systems is more significant than a morphological one, as the type of cave passage depends considerably on local geology. Most systems contain both phreatic and vadose sections, in a ratio determined largely by age. Many of the high level abandoned phreatic systems are earlier than at least the last glacial, as they are often choked with glacial deposits. There is thus a strong contrast between high-level, pre-main glacial and low-level, post-main glacial cave systems.

Caves tend to decrease in size upstream and they appear to enlarge from the bottom up. Cave collapse is only a secondary process, when systems are already well developed. Many of the young vadose caves show no signs of collapse, although it has occurred in the Lancaster Ease Gill caves. Phreatic drainage was dominant in preglacial times, and was dominated by hydraulic conditions, so that passages were directed towards the major risings along the maximum hydraulic gradients. Vadose systems on the other hand, are determined by geological factors that determine the easiest routes. Five factors are important, (a) shale beds, of which there are more than 20 in the Great Scar limestone, (b) variations in lithology, (c) gentle folds, which occur in the Ingleborough area, (d) joints and (e) faults. The Lost Johns master cave is the largest example of the first control. Leck Fell has a synclinal system. Joints are particularly deep near the North

Craven fault, and deep caves occur here as on Newby Moss. In contrast in Penyghent Gill, where caves are shallow and horizontal, joints rarely penetrate more than about 4 m. Meregill Hole and Birks Fell cave illustrate fault guided caves. Large, enterable caves only form where surface drainage is concentrated into a sizeable stream, which occurs on shale outcrops. The lack of large through systems around Ingleborough is due to the vadose underground drainage being largely north down the dip, while the major resurgences are at the southern margin of the area, where the surface drainage is southwards. Thus much of the phreatic drainage is against the dip.

Cave chronology is difficult to assess quantitatively (Waltham 1974), although the Morecambe Bay area offers the best conditions. In northwest Yorkshire the Victoria Cave [840650] contains a Middle Pleistocene fauna of hippopotamus, elephant and rhinoceros. The large surface depression around High Mark is probably of Tertiary date. However, most of the karst features are much younger, dating only from the Devensian and Flandrian. Caves show evidence of alternating erosion and deposition, related to strong climatic variation. Solutional activity and new sink initiation took place mainly in colder phases, by the action of meltwater. Rejuvenation of phreatic caves is related to the lowering of resurgence levels resulting from glacial erosion of the valleys, although it is difficult to avoid circular reasoning as the caves provide the best evidence for valley incision.

Examples of specific caves systems Four different types of cave system are exemplified by specific caves. The Morecambe Bay area illustrates the characteristics of the older cave systems, developed close to the sea; the Leck Fell cave system is an example of a fairly simple cave; while the caves of Kingsdale illustrate the effects of glacial activity; and finally the Gaping Gill system is unique and one of the best known in the Northern England area.

Caves in the Morecambe Bay area are mostly dry and fossilised, as they have lost their impervious capping. They are unusual and show a type of phreatic development unique in Northern England. The limestone is cut by faults that moved at the close of the Carboniferous period, and to the north the New Red sandstone overlaps the older rocks. The period of maximum erosion was during the Permian, at the time of the Hercynian uplift, when caves would have developed. Haematite iron ore filled some caves where they were covered by New Red sandstone. The present relief represents an exhumed Permo-Triassic topography, modified by Miocene faulting and glaciation. Cave formation was extensive, and is now recognisable by infill. There are three cave types in the Morecambe Bay area, (a) phreatic networks, (b) abandoned vadose caves and (c) abandoned sea caves. The limestones have fairly steep dips and shakeholes are rare owing to the lack of drift, but there are dolines and uvalas. There may even be true poljes, for example Hale Moss [505773]. They are probably interglacial in origin. Four main phreatic networks are known in different rock types; in Roudsea Wood caves the rock is oolitic limestone, while the Hazel Grove caves are in standard limestone. They are horizontal even in dipping limestone, and are associated with closed depressions. Solutional forms are common, showing limited vadose activity. Roudsea Wood [328810] caves in the Leven Estuary have two main passage systems, 600 m long in all. The passages are oval and horizontal in limestone dipping at 15 degrees, indicating water level control by a proglacial lake or estuary. Some originally phreatic caves have been modified by vadose activity. They occur in glacial meltwater channels and were abandoned when the water supply ceased; they are at the boundary of impermeable rocks, as in the Henning valley west of Lindal [250757]. Caves in the Kellet area [520700] were of phreatic origin, then modified by vadose activity with infill and collapse also taking place. They indicate a past base-level of 80 m. They are in meltwater valleys. Old sea caves occur at former sea-levels, as given by Parry (1960), for example Whitbarrow cave [440870] at 115 m, and Harry Hest Hole on Warton Crag [490730] also at 115 m. No others occur above 30 m, but at this level Kirkland cave has archaeological material; it was probably enlarged by marine erosion in the Devensian (Würm) 2 a/b interstadial. The postglacial transgression has eroded caves near Silverdale [460755]. Levels at which caves occur include 5 m, 15 m, 20 m, 30 m (P. Ashmead 1974).

On Leck Fell on the western flanks of Gragareth a whole
series of caves that are interrelated have been described by A.C.
Waltham (1974). The Lost Johns Cave [671787] is the most extensive, and Pippikin Hole is another. There are 10 km of known
passages in 1 km² block of limestone. Pippikin Hole is less then
1 km from the Dent fault. The limestone is covered by till, but
there is no surface drainage except in very wet weather on the
till. There are many shake holes in the till, but only a few exceed
15 m across. The caves show a multiphase development, each
having a lower resurgence level, so that vadose erosion gets pro-
gressively deeper. There are three erosion phases separated by
two periods of calcite deposition and sediment infilling. The last
phase of erosion is the present one. The first phase created large
phreatic tubes. In Pippikin Hole there are nearly 7 km of passages
with a vertical range of 110 m. The main passage is an abandoned
phreatic tunnel from The Hobbit to Gour Hall, it is 6 m in diameter and belongs to the first phase. There was then vadose rejuvenation in phase 3, following clastic fill and calcite formation.
There are many stalagmites. Further passages developed in the
fifth phase, including Cigatere Passage, where the main stream
now flows. Undercutting and collapse linked the old phreatic
tunnel to the younger streamways. The cave systems of this area
are illustrated in fig. 3.3a & b.

A little south of the Leck Fell system are the Kingsdale Caves,
which are complex. They consist of abandoned phreatic tunnels,
vadose shafts and deep pitches (D. Brook 1974). Jingling Pot is
on a master joint [699784] , and has a 30 m pitch. The caves
probably developed when the limestone was exposed by erosion
following uplift in Tertiary times. The linear valley is probably
structurally guided, but has since been modified by glaciation to
become wider, deeper and straighter. Large surface streams from
the Yoredale strata invaded the original micro-phreatic network
and rapid phreatic enlargement occurred. The system became
vadose as the system drained more freely, with vadose pitches
linking phreatic zones, until the whole became vadose. Capture
and short circuiting took place. Swinsto long crawl is a 300 m
long bedding plane passage, enlarged by retreating vadose
trenches. Joints and bedding have controlled the Kingsdale

system. The Pleistocene ice advances have been responsible for the cave development and most of the caves started to form under former ice sheets. The older sinks were probably initiated subglacially in West Kingsdale. Temporary lakes formed during

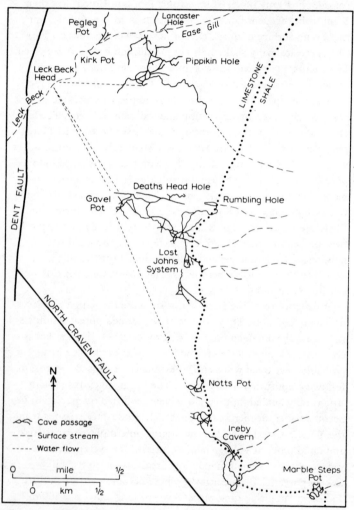

Fig. 3.3 *Above* a) The caves of Leck Fell and western Gragareth. *Opposite* b) Plan of Pippikin Hole caves.

glacial retreat, and these also played an important part. Till
choked some cave entrances, while fluvioglacial deposits have influenced cave development, as shingle helps with the corrasion of
vadose channels. The drowning of stalactites indicates a raising of
the water level in Keld Head, due to the filling of an old lake. In
other areas fluvioglacial floor deposits prevent solution or corrasion, and fine particles settle in dammed up sections, often
resting on coarser sediments, giving for example, the Mud River
Series in Rowton Pot. The cave pattern is illustrated in fig. 3.3c.

The Gaping Gill system, described by R.R. Glover (1974)
drains Fell Beck. The cave system is illustrated in plan and
section in fig. 3.4a and b Fell Beck has cut into the drift, its blind
valley ending with a 10 m high slope, and then it drops 110 m to
the Main Chamber. Salt experiments in 1904 showed that Fell
Beck emerged at Clapham Beck Head after 11 days, with the
maximum salt concentration occurring after 14 days, the water
having covered 1.5 km. Flood water passes through the system at
a greater speed in only a few hours.

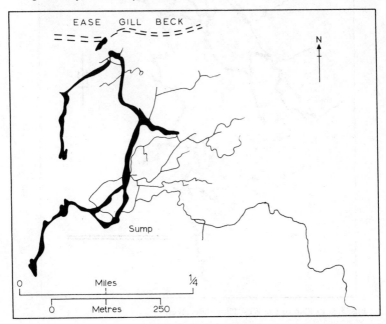

There are five other entrances to the system, which is more than 10 km long. There are independent vertical and horizontal portions, and massive clastic accumulation. The horizontal passages

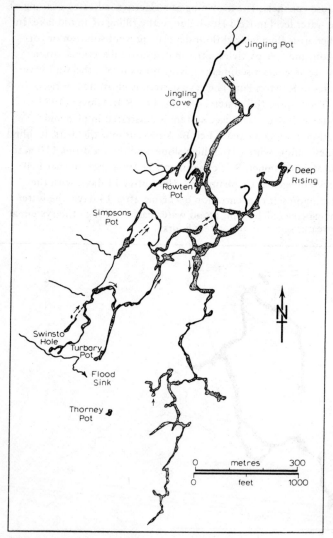

Fig. 3.3 c) Plan of the West Kingsdale caves.

are at 3 to 4 levels, mostly about 110 m below the moor level, or about 300 m O.D. There are many shafts. The system can be divided into five morphological types: (a) vadose inlets include shafts, potholes and sinkholes. The main shaft is joint controlled, and Disappointment Pot is another in this category. (b) Aven

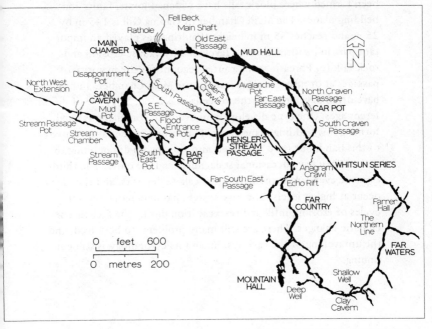

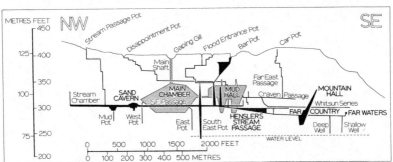

Fig. 3.4 *Top a)* Plan of the Gaping Gill cave system. *Above b)* Diagrammatic cross section of the main passages of the Gaping Gill system.

systems are clearing mud and sand fill in places, and lie along bedding planes. They are now vadose inlets, but have had a long history, and may have acted as phreatic risers. (c) Vadose trunk routes include Hensler's Stream Passage, which only carries much water in flood periods at present. (d) Very large chambers have been formed where block falls have widened joints, faults and bedding planes. The Main Chamber of Gaping Gill is 145 m by 25 m and reaches 35 m in height. Faulting has played an important part in its formation. It developed by vadose erosion and rock fall. (e) Phreatic trunk routes account for the majority of passages at or near the floor level of the Main Chamber, and they have often developed on the Porcellanous band. They are of different ages. One type developed on or in the Porcellanous band, forming low bedding plane caves. The second type is also related to this band, but they are larger, also flowing up-dip or along the strike. They have occasional stalagmites and are older. The third type are even larger and have more calcite deposits, and they may occur at higher levels. The cave system has undergone several cycles of erosion, infill and re-excavation during the Pleistocene climatic changes. There are still many problems to be solved, and the unravelling of the cave system and its chronology is still continuing.

4   Glaciation

The details of the landscape of the whole of Northern England
have been markedly affected by glaciation. In order to discuss the
effect of the ice age on the area a brief summary of some aspects
of a possible glacial sequence will be given first, followed by a
description of the results of glacial erosion, glacial deposition and
glaci-fluvial activity. It is not possible to give a detailed description of the glaciation of the whole area only examples of the
various effects of glaciation in different parts.

Glacial chronology
Over much of Northern England the evidence of the earlier
phases of the glacial period have been obliterated by the later
advances, which have left the most conspicuous glacial features.
The fullest evidence of the glacial succession is found in borings
made through the glacial deposits of the northern part of the Isle
of Man, where the drift is over 150 m thick. There are three
layers of till, each overlain by stratified sands and gravels, with
marine sands and silts lying between the lowest and middle set.
The uppermost series builds the very conspicuous Bride moraine.
The section is shown in fig. 2.6 line EF.

Wolstonian It is thought that the lowest unit of the northern Isle
of Man glacial sequence can be correlated with the Early Scottish
glaciation of Edenside, described by Trotter (1929b). It has also
been correlated with the Eastern General drift of Ireland
(Cubbon 1954-6). This would put the earliest recorded glaciation
over most of Northern England into the youngest of the Older
Drift sequence, the Wolstonian, the equivalent of the Saale on
the continent.

At that time it is probable that nearly all of Northern England was mantled by ice. There is evidence in the Lake District and the Pennines of high level drift, now found as erratics carried above their natural outcrop. The finer material has been removed from these deposits, which are now often covered by peat. This glaciation is known as the Maximum Lake District and Maximum Dales glaciation.

During the Wolstonian glaciation ice moved southwards from Scotland up the Eden valley, bringing Scottish erratics southwards, thus indicating the relatively great power of the Scottish ice compared with the Lake District ice during this period (see fig. 4.1). There is also evidence of powerful ice in the Irish Sea at this time, as the whole of the mountain group of the Isle of Man may have been over-run by ice, local ice combining with far-travelled ice. The Scandinavian drift of the Northumberland and Durham coasts probably dates from this relatively early glacial period, showing that a powerful ice stream from Scandinavia filled the North Sea at this time. Till of this age in County Durham is now only found at one locality in Warren House Gill [448442], where it was described by Trechmann (1952) but it is now largely buried under coal-mine debris. Thus during the earliest ice advance that has left a record of its presence in the area, powerful ice streams, coming particularly from the north, and impinging on the coast from Scandinavia, covered much of the area. This ice presumably caused considerable erosion, although it is difficult in many areas to differentiate its erosional effects from those of the later periods.

Last Interglacial The succeeding interglacial period is indicated by the marine deposits at the Point of Ayre in the Isle of Man and by interglacial deposits containing an ox tooth near Appleby in the Eden valley. Little is known at present, however, of geomorphological events connected with this period of deglaciation, which is the Last Interglacial or Ipswichian (Eemian).

Devensian

Lake District and Pennines The Devensian Glaciation (last or

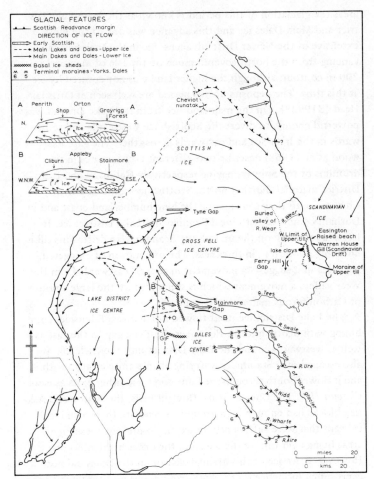

Fig. 4.1 Directions of ice movement at different stages of glaciation and at different positions within the ice sheet. Other glacial features are also indicated. (Insets based on the work of S.E. Hollingworth.)

Weichsel) has left the most important effects of glacial activity in the area. These later ice advance obliterated much of the earlier evidence and they were certainly responsible for many of the present details of the landscape in such areas as the Lake District and Pennine Dales where ice was particularly active. In these areas the glaciation of this period is known as the Main Lake District and Main Dales ice and this advance was one of the most extensive of the Newer Drift advances. Ice in the Irish Sea advancing from the north covered much of the Isle of Man up to 200 m contour, although the higher land was not covered by ice at this time. The deposits of this period are well seen at Orrisdale Head [319928]. On the mainland, ice from the Lake District was powerful enough to divert the Scottish ice westwards and southwards in the Irish Sea and eastwards across the Tyne gap. Eastwood et al. (1968) describe two different erratic suites in the drumlins of the Solway, having respectively Galloway and Lake District material. Further north, Scottish ice combined with Cheviot ice to flow south along the Northumberland coast and in Durham combined with local Pennine and Lake District ice. It left a layer of till on the underlying Scandinavian drift. This till is normally about 6 m in thickness. The orientation of elongated particles in it suggests a movement in general eastwards from the Wear valley, a movement which is supported by the large amount of Carboniferous material in the till.

The Lake District ice itself flowed north down Edenside, combining with Scottish ice to flow over the Tyne gap to the east as well as westwards round the Lake District into the Irish Sea. It also escaped over Stainmore, carrying Shap granite erratics with it, and it flowed south through the Lune gorge and other exits as well. *Cheviot Hills* The Cheviot Hills, Howgill Fells, the Alston and Askrigg blocks had enough high ground to generate their own local ice caps that were sufficiently powerful to prevent these high areas being over-run by the ice from the other highland centres. However active ice of this Main glaciation in the Dales did not exert much influence on the high ground, but was confined to the valleys. The ice was not a very effective agent of erosion apart from a few exceptional areas. This also applies to the Howgill Fells, the Alston block and the Cheviot Hills, the reason being the blockage of the free outlets for the local ice by ice from the more important highland centres. The problem of the existence of an ice cap over the Cheviot Hills has been studied by C.M. Clapperton (1970a). The evidence for the ice cap includes alignment of meltwater channels, glacial striae, occurrence of erratics,

moraines and erosional features. The pattern suggests radial outflow from the centre of the Cheviot massif and the hills to the
west, while the ground below 300 m was occupied by Tweed ice
to the north and Solway ice to the south, the three ice masses
being confluent. The Cheviot Hills reach 816 m, with 2.5 km^2
above 760 m, but on the higher ground evidence of glaciation is
less obvious than below 300 m. Erratics have been recorded up to
580 m. Striations although not common, suggest radial outflow
from the high ground. Marginal meltwater channels have an upper
limit, and form two sets converging from northeast and southeast
on the Breamish valley. They fall in elevation from about 365 m
in the west to 180 m near the Breamish valley. They are related
to the far-travelled ice that surrounded the hills. There are few
meltwater channels in the western part of the massif, but some
occur in the higher eastern part; these often have up and down
profiles suggesting sub- and en-glacial features, cut as the ice
wasted down. They are generally aligned down valley and require
local ice on the hills to explain their pattern. Some valleys show
signs of glacial erosion, such as those draining north to the Lambden valley, including College Burn, Goldscleugh, Bellyside and
Bizzle valleys. The Bizzle amphitheatre is probably a cirque, and
moraines have been identified in it. These date from the lateglacial and suggest former larger glaciers. Tors occur, but these
cannot be considered as evidence of non-glaciation.

The maximum of the Main glaciation advance can probably be
correlated with the lower part of the Devensian. However the
complexity of the Newer Drift period is becoming increasingly
apparent. There were several interstadial recessions and subsequent advances that have yet to be fully worked out and correlated. It appears that one of the earlier and more important of
these readvances was the Scottish Readvance phase, during which
ice advanced south of the Scottish border to the neighbourhood
of Carlisle and Brampton on the west where it reached the 125 m
contour line (see fig. 4.1), and valley glaciers developed in the
Lake District. Some of these were large enough to form piedmont
lobes, with which drumlins are associated.

Isle of Man The Isle of Man provides a very complex set of glacial deposits, which indicate possible interpretations of the glacial chronology in the area. Mitchell (1971) has described the glacial succession on the west coast of the island. At Glen Mooar [302893] Ballateare gravels are intruded by tongues of Mooar till, which is possibly of Devensian age, although previously Mitchell has considered it to be Wolstonian in age. The Ballateare till is brown and shelly, and is truncated by the sands and gravels of Orrisdale age, which is definitely considered Devensian in age. The Orrisdale till is red, sandy and calcareous, with local and distant erratics and some shells. It is overlain by lateglacial deposits, in which a date of 12,000 BP has been recorded. At Orrisdale Head [319928] till is overlain by gravels, which become coarser and thicker northwards, with fine sands coming in on top. Mitchell comes to the conclusion that there are two shelly tills in the Irish Sea, the earlier is definitely Wolstonian, but the upper, including the Ballateare till, could well be Devensian.

A well-developed alluvial fan with kettle holes occurs at the mouth of Glen Dhoo, near Ballaugh [347936]. Zone II pollen occurs at the base of the infill and zone III climatic deterioration is indicated by changes in the pollen. Dates of 11,350 BP and 12,150 BP have been obtained from the lining of kettle holes at the base of Glen Wyllin [310907] alluvial fan. More recently R. Coope has obtained a date of 18,990 ± 300 BP from the very base of the organic layer, below the level sampled by Mitchell. This date sets an upper limit to the formation of the Bride moraine, as the kettle hole lies just in front of the moraine. The kettle hole does not appear to have been overrun by ice since its formation. South of Glen Mooar [302893] the Mooar till rests on Ballateare till, although in places the two are intermixed. The Mooar till is probably part of the Manx upland deposits that are probably periglacial in origin. These deposits intermix with foreign derived till at the margin of foreign ice incursion.

On the east coast at Ballure [459935] G.S.P. Thomas (1971) describes the section in which 14 stratigraphic units, including five tills, gravels and clays, occur. The deposits, as on the west coast, show a mixture of local and foreign material, the latter including outwash and the former local slope and flood deposits. The Dog Mills outwash series, which outcrops along the coast between Ramsey and Shellag Point, immediately predate the formation of the Bride moraine. They are the equivalent of the upper red clays at Ballure. All the deposits on the east coast are considered to be of Devensian (Weichselian) age. There is some evidence for Eemian raised beach deposits, as rounded erratics occur in scree deposits overlying the old cliff and platform.

The Ayre drift plain consists of up to 180 m of drift. At the highest point the Bride moraine reaches over 92 m O.D., and is underlain by 46 m of drift. The solid rock is found at −125 m O.D. at the Point of Ayre. A 7 km section of cliffs, cut in the drift, between Dog Mills [453978] and Phurt [468027], reveals proglacial outwash deposits, moraine, readvance tills and other deposits, including raised beach deposits that lap onto the glacial sequence in the north. There are 15 stratigraphical units representing four alternating tills and sands. The lowest till is the Shellag-Kionlough till, followed by the Ballavarkish, Ballaquark and the Cranstal tills upwards. The Dog Mills deposits are outwash, while to the north increasing tectonic disturbance distorts the stratigraphy, and includes thrusts, folds and faults. Three major tectonic disturbances occur at the height of the moraine near Shellag Point [461000]. The major structures show planes dipping up-glacier, which is the opposite direction demanded by the push moraine hypothesis. G.S.P. Thomas suggests tentatively that some overriding features are present, followed by ice retreat and outwash formation, giving the Shellag gravels, which are associated with the Ballavarkish till. He suggests that melting of dead ice in the Shellag till, underlying the Shellag gravels, caused slumping, slip and shear between the till and gravels, clay being injected up into the gravels. The moraine formed probably during the readvance of the ice that deposited the Ballavarkish till. This ice also disturbed the deposits north of Shellag Point. The Ballavarkish till was in turn disturbed by the advance of the Ballaquark ice. The lowest Shellag till is probably the equivalent of the Orrisdale deposits on the west coast. The Bride moraine is probably a terminal feature and not a retreat stage. The Cranstal till may be the ablation moraine of the Ballaquark till. The age of the Ballavarkish till probably lies between a lower limit of 25,000 BP and an upper limit of 19,000 BP, if Coope's date of 18,990 is reliable. It should be stressed that this chronology is very tentative at present.

Durham One of the features of the glaciation of the Durham area is the complex system of buried valleys, now filled with drift. There are three separate systems, one in the west draining to the Wear system, an eastern coastal system, and a southern system associated with the Tees. The Durham area can be divided into four subdivisions in terms of the glacial deposits. The Wear valley forms the western area, the central one is based on the Permian plateau, the eastern one on the 3-13 km coastal strip, and the southern one on the Tees valley, south of Ferry Hill.

There is evidence in the east for three glaciations. Scandinavian drift is overlain by Lower gravels, Lower till, Middle sands in two divisions, Upper till, moraine and Upper gravels and finally prismatic clay. In the central area the lowest and most extensive deposit is the Lower till, which is up to 36 m thick. Laminated clays up to 50 m occur at many points in the Edder Acres and Wingate area in a depression on the till. The clay is bounded on the east by the Upper till 1.5 to 15 m thick, and by moraine which may overlie the clay in places. Sands and gravels are also associated with the clay and occur in meltwater channels, which drained the lake in which the clays accumulated. In the southern area there is a tripartite division, of Lower till, Middle sands and Upper till. The Lower till has Shap granite pebbles. The same tripartite pattern occurs in the western area, where the Middle sands also include gravels and clays up to 80 m thick, and these deposits are bedded and laminated in places.

The chronology suggested by the Geological Survey (Smith and Francis 1967) begins with an early incursion of Scandinavian till a short distance inland. Norwegian erratics occur in Warren House Gill. The Lower till which contains Lake District, Southern Uplands and Cheviot erratics was deposited by a major ice sheet moving south or southeast. In the eastern area the lower part of the Middle sands is thought to be outwash of the waning Lower till ice, much water was available, channels were cut and coarse sediments laid down in them. A longish interval intervened before the Upper Middle sands were deposited, during which the

Easington raised beach may have formed. In the western area most of the Middle sands, gravels and clay belong to the decay of the Lower till ice.

The Upper till ice and Upper Middle sands came from the north and the ice moved inland only to the 125 m contour, leaving a north-south moraine ridge from Easington to Hutton Henry. This till is certainly Devensian in age. The moraine dammed the Edder Acres Lake, which extended to Sheraton. The Upper Stony till of the western area probably belongs to the Lower till ice episode, possibly being due to a local readvance.

There are problems concerning the date of the Lower till. It overlies loess and is post-Hoxnian, and probably equivalent of the Drab till of Holderness, which Penny has dated as Main Würm or Late Devensian. The Easington raised beach evidence suggests a Gipping age for the Lower till, although the Upper till is definitely Devensian and is the equivalent of the Hessle and Hunstanton tills. The Upper till is overlain at Neasham with Zone I clays without a break.

The minimum age of the Easington raised beach is 38,000 yr BP; shells in the beach deposit at Shippersea [443453] have provided the date. It is thought to be interglacial and not interstadial on account of its fauna. The beach must, therefore, be pre-Devensian, and not younger than Ipswichian. On the evidence of pebbles in the beach, the Lower till should be older than the beach, as the pebbles in the beach were probably derived from the Lower till.

P. Beaumont (1970) suggests that both the tills probably belong to the Devensian, during which Cheviot ice was forced onshore by the pressure of ice in the North Sea, probably after the ice that laid down the Lower till had stagnated. The later ice sheet then stagnated itself.

Lancashire Plain The pattern of glacial deposits in the Lancashire Plain is fairly consistent, but the interpretation of their origin has been much debated, and rival suggestions and dates have been put forward. The sequence consists in many places of three units, which are a Lower till, an intermediate layer of deposits known as the Middle sands, and an Upper till. The controversy has centred on whether these deposits represent two distinct glacial advances, with the Middle sands representing at least an interstadial, or whether the whole sequence belongs to one complex phase of glacial deposition.

B.J. Taylor (1958) showed that the two tills are widespread. He considered that the first glacial period was a major one, with ice extending up to nearly 400 m on the Pennine flanks, southeast of Stockport. Sands outcrop at 183 m near Whirley Grove [885747] where their structure shows signs of stress. They are overlain by Upper till, and show disturbance by folding and tilting, with minor thrusting and shear planes, the latter being followed by cemented veins. The throws are normal. It is suggested that the faulting was caused by pressure of overlying ice. Iron oxide has migrated towards the more closely packed sand along the shear planes.

The deposits in the Manchester area between Hyde [960950], Fallowfield [855945], and Cheadle Hulme [868862], in the north, and High Lane [960855] in the south, have been described by I.M. Simpson (1959). The area covers the Mersey valley, which is terraced. The tripartite arrangement of the glacial strata is recognised in the area, the Lower till, Middle sands and Upper till are overlain by the upper sand and gravels of the river terraces. The Lower till is a stiff, dark-brown clay with scattered pebbles. It includes lenticular sand beds from 1.5 to 6 m thick. The average thickness of the Lower till is 15 m, but it varies from zero to more than 24 m. The Middle sands dip with the Lower till to the west. The sands attain a thickness of 15 m on Heaton Moor [872918], but elsewhere they are only 3.7 m thick. They contain well rounded pebbles. The contact between the Middle sands and the Upper till is very irregular in places, for example at Bramhall [892860]. The higher ground is covered by the Upper till above 70 m in the southwest and 90 m in the east. The lithology of the Lower and Upper tills is similar, and they both contain shells, derived from the floor of the Irish Sea. Where the Middle sands are missing it is impossible to separate the two tills. It appears that the Middle sands were frozen and eroded before the Upper till was laid down in some places, although in others the two deposits are conformable.

There are four terraces in the Mersey Valley at 2.4, 4.6, 6.1 and 10.7 m above the normal river level. The highest is the most extensive. Two of the terraces north of Woodley slope at 5.15 m/km, which is the same as the regional dip of the glacial deposits. The terraces are due to changes in load and volume in the river, rather than to changes in sea level. There is some evidence for the presence of a lake after the ice that deposited the Upper till retreated. One of the most controversial sites is that at Chelford [SJ 812731], 19 km south of Stockport, where plant remains from the Middle sands have been dated at 47,000 yr $^{+2300}_{-1800}$ BP. The pollen belongs to the early Devensian, more specifically to the Brørup, an early, cool interstadial within it (Shotton *et al.* 1970, pp. 385-6).

I.M. Simpson (1960) suggests that all of the threefold succession probably belongs to the Newer Drift (Devensian) period. The organic remains from the Middle sands suggests a milder interstadial. He has also analysed the stone content of the clays. The range of erratics from four different localities were all similar. The Lower till gave 16% dark sandstone, 11% fine-grained igneous material, 26% light sandstone, 8% shale and mudstone, and 7% clay ironstone. The Middle sands yielded 20% dark sandstone, 12% fine-grained igneous rocks, 45% light sandstone and 6.6% vein quartz. Many of the erratics come from the Millstone Grit Series. The Upper till could not be distinguished from the Lower on the basis of erratics, and therefore could be the product of one complex glacial episode. The stone content of the Middle sands differs on account of the different environment of deposition, the softer rocks being lacking. Simpson suggests that the Middle sands are the outwash of the retreating Lower till ice and the advancing Upper till ice.

The simple tripartite division of the Lancashire Plain drift is not ubiquitous. P.M. Mather (1969) quotes a number of borehole logs, which were made in connection with motorway construction, in which several layers of clay with intervening sands occur. The Middle sands are by no means continuous and represent heterogeneous and discontinuous deposits that probably accumulated in a variety of depositional environments. This was recog-

nised by Thompson and Worsley (1966), who considered that the
Middle sands and the two tills occurred within a single stagnating
ice sheet. R.H. Johnson (1965) also subscribes to the view that
the deposits belong to one complex glaciation, with the sequence
being the result of oscillations of the ice front prior to final dissi-
pation. Further south the Middle sands have been recognised as
belonging to two phases, the lower indicating westerly flow and
including wind-blown sands, while the upper one shows indication of southerly flow (Evans *et al.* 1968). This succession may
also apply in the Lancashire Plain, although there is little direct
evidence that this is so.

There are few radiometric dates of the drifts from the Lancashire area itself, the Chelford deposit being the nearest. Dates
from shells at the base of upper of the two sand divisions, the
Gawsworth sand, recognised by Evans *et al.* give 28,000 +1800-
1500 BP (Boulton and Worsley 1965). This date suggests that the
major advance of the Irish Sea ice was later than this. The conclusion reached by Evans *et al.* (1968) and Mather (1969) is that
the main Irish Sea ice advance took place between 25,000 and
16,000 BP, reaching a maximum about 20,000 BP, and that only
the lower part of the Middle sands, from which the Chelford date
was obtained, and the Lower till, which is probably rather limited
in extent and not necessarily inclusive of all the till below sand
deposits, belongs to an earlier period of glaciation, possibly
Wolstonian, and the equivalent of the Basement till of Holderness
and the lower till of the Durham area.

Gresswell (1967) described the glacial sequence in the Fylde
area to the north of the Ribble. He has shown that a similar
sequence occurs in this area to that described in the Lancashire
Plain further south. The till in the Fylde is red in colour, indicating that much erosion of the New Red sandstone took place
by ice action, the material being subsequently incorporated into
the drifts of the Fylde area. The glacial sequence again consists
of the tripartite division of Upper and Lower tills separated by
Middle sands. The sands in this area also are lenticular in form
and occur at different horizons. Gresswell agrees with the view
that the deposits could all belong to one complex phase of deglaciation.

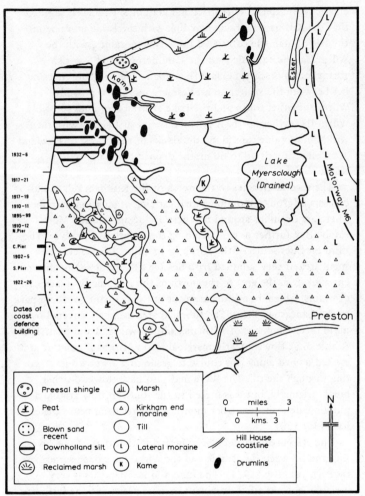

Fig. 4.2 Some features of the geomorphology of the Fylde. (After R.K. Gresswell.)

Three areas are distinguished. Firstly there is a discontinuous multiple ridge running from Singleton [385383] to Kirkham [425320], (fig. 4.2). This is a complex end moraine, including deposits of clays, sands and gravels. There are peaty hollows such as Marton Mere [342353] near Blackpool, and rocks include

erratics from the Lake District and Pennines. Gresswell suggests
that the Kirkham moraine may link with the Bride moraine in
the Isle of Man. He correlated these two moraines, with the
Würm IIa, the equivalent of the Lammermuir and Scottish
Readvance moraines, i.e. late Devensian. The Kirkham moraine
lies between the Whitchurch-Ellesmere moraines (possibly
Würm I) further south and the Lake District moraines (possibly
Würm II) further north. A lateral moraine associated with the
Kirkham moraine runs along the flanks of the Forest of Bowland
at an elevation of 46 to 60 m, the deposit being up to 38 m
thick.

The second area lies to the north of the Kirkham ridges and
consists of ground moraine with a capping of ablation moraine.
There are drumlins around northern Fylde and around Morecambe Bay further north, including the mouth of the Wyre. The
third area lies south of the Kirkham moraine. It consists of a
small area of very subdued Irish Sea Ice till, and it can be differentiated from the area to the north of the moraine by a lack of
drumlins, which do not occur in south Fylde or the southern part
of the Lancashire Plain. The subdued area is largely covered by
more recent deposits of saltmarsh silt, blown sand and peat. The
Ribble once flowed nearly marginal to the Kirkham moraine and
eroded its bed along this course to grade to a lower sea-level, cutting through the till. The Wyre may also have flowed further
north originally, but was forced to the south to flow around a
morainic deposit. Its earlier mouth may have been near Cocker-
ham [450520].

The effects of the last glacial period in that part of northwest
England between the Ribble and the Wirral have been summarised
by R.H. Johnson (1971). The succession of deposits is very
variable, but one till is dominant in most parts, with underlying
and/or overlying sands and gravels. Locally, however, five tills
exist, indicating complex local events. In a few places an older till
can be seen, and this is probably of Wolstonian age. In other areas
till can be shown to be diachronous with regard to the sands and
gravels. Most of the deposits are Devensian in age and much of
the till is derived from local rocks. Some of the till is tough and
dense, but most is melt-out till, which is wetter, more permeable

and oxidises more readily. These tills deform easily under stress. The massive sand and gravel deposits indicate much fluvioglacial material. There is also evidence of active ice in the drumlins, with relatively little stagnant decaying ice. The north Lancashire and Cheshire ground moraine is associated with actively moving ice.

The evidence for chronology suggests a full-glacial period from 20,000 to 16,000 BP. The Main Irish Sea Ice culminated about 20,000 years ago after the build up of ice in Scotland and the Lake District from 25,000 B.P. The Main Irish Sea Ice reached Wolverhampton about 20,000 years ago, while the Kirkham and Whitchurch moraine is the equivalent in time of the Bride moraine in the Isle of Man, forming a short time before 16,000 B.P. The York moraine is of similar age. The Bølling interstadial is dated at 12,400 to 12,000 B.P. and is thought of as the early part of the Allerød period, which lasted from 11,950 to 10,800 B.P. From 10,800 to 10,300 there was a colder spell, when kettle moraine related to stagnant ice formed at the head of Haweswater and elsewhere in the Lake District.

In the subsequent period terraces were aggraded in the Mersey and Weaver catchments (R.H. Johnson 1969-70). The Mersey High terrace was aggraded at the close of the Late-glacial about 8500 B.P. and completed in 3000 years. This datum is common to all the valleys investigated. Erosion of this terrace and the formation of the younger ones was influenced by sea-level changes, although climatic changes, by controlling stream discharge and load, were more important. Knick-points were formed, but have had no time to retreat. They occur where the streams became superimposed on the bedrock below the drift and are fossilised in these positions, only retreating upstream very slowly.

Lateglacial moraines There have been several later stages of advance and retreat of the ice fronts. One advance belongs to the colder phase of Zone I when glaciers again formed in the Lake District hills. Evidence of them is given by their end moraines, for example that of the Coniston valley is at Nibthwaite [294897] and that of the Windermere valley is at Haverthwaite [340840]. This period of colder conditions was followed by the milder Allerød period of Zone II covering the years from about 11,950 to 10,750 B.P. This period has been fairly accurately fixed by radiocarbon dating. A date from the top of an organic layer of this Zone II period at Lunds [789952] (Walker 1955b) (see fig. 4.2) gives 10,592 BP ±120 years. Lateglacial organic deposits in the Isle of Man, accumulating in basins amongst ridges formed by the retreat of the ice depositing the Orrisdale series have yielded 14C dates ranging between 12,150 and 10,250 BP (Mitchell 1965). These lie mainly within the Allerød period. The deposits were later buried to a depth of 13 m by sands and gravels released by the melting of permafrost and washed down to form an early postglacial alluvial fan at the mouth of Glen Wyllin. A Zone II date of 11,942 ±120 BP has also been obtained for a sample of detritus mud from Low Wray Bay at the northern end of Lake Windermere [376014].

The final lateglacial formation of ice in Northern England took place between 10,750 and 10,250 BP (Zone III). Small corrie glaciers developed in the Lake District, for example at Hartrigg in the Kent valley [457060] there is a moraine dating from this final ice advance in the district. There may also have been small corrie glaciers in the high Cross Fell hills. However, elsewhere in Northern England there was probably no ice, only semi-permanent snow patches, for example on the higher ground of the western Askrigg block in the upper Eden valley and also in the Cheviots, where there was no ice at this time. The deterioration of climate in the post-Allerød period has been studied by G. Manley (1959). From a study of the geomorphology of the Lake District and north Pennine moraines of this stage he considers that the cold spell lasting from 10,750 to 10,150 BP was associated with a 4 to 5°C fall of mean temperature. The climate was probably cloudy and damp in summer, thus reducing ablation and allowing glacial maxima, but the duration of the cold phase was short, resulting in limited glacier growth.

These later ice advances did not cover the hills of the Isle of Man, which has too maritime and mild a climate to nourish its own glaciers except during the most severe glacial periods. The paucity of glaciated features in the island is particularly striking when it is compared with the Lake District which is so close.

D. Walker (1966b) has shown by pollen analysis that the Zone

III glacial features in the Langdale valley extended as low as 120 m O.D. at the head of Great Langdale and to 230 m in Kentmere. Kettle moraines associated with dead ice do not, however, all belong necessarily to this period of ice advance. Ice began to accumulate for the Zone III advance after 10,870 BP ±120 years in upper Langdale.

Table 4.1 shows a possible correlation within the district and with neighbouring areas, but it must be stressed that this is no more than a working hypothesis that will be modified as further evidence is found.

Glacial erosion

A glacier's capacity to erode depends very much on the speed of flow and the ice thickness, thus the greatest effects of glacial erosion are found where the ice was well nourished and had a relatively free outlet allowing it to flow fast. Steeper gradients also enhanced the rate of flow.

Lake District The area where glacial erosion has been most conspicuously significant in modifying the landscape of Northern England was in the Lake District. This area, because of its westerly situation and high elevation, receives a heavy precipitation. Borrowdale (Seathwaite) has 3000 mm/yr precipitation, the value increasing to 4600 mm below Great End. When more of this fell as snow it would have produced a thick and active ice sheet. The outlets from the Lake District were numerous and the slopes steep so that the ice attained a considerable thickness and velocity down the steep gradients, particularly where it was concentrated in the valleys. Linton (1957) has shown how the radial pattern of glacial troughs has developed as a result of radial flow in all directions away from the main ice cap centre.

In the Lake District features associated with glacial erosion are very well developed. There are many corries, a considerable number of which contain lakes. Blea Water [448108] beneath High Street has been taken by Lewis (1960) as a typical example of a well-developed corrie basin with a lake. Red Tarn [347153] below Helvellyn is another good example. In this vicinity glacial sapping of the corrie side wall has produced the arête feature of

Quaternary correlation table

Isle of Man		Isle of Man	Lake District	Pennines
West coast (Mitchell)	*East coast* (Thomas)	(Cubbon)	(Trotter and Hollingworth & others)	(Raistrick & others)
Kettle hole fill Zone II Ballaugh fan		Solifluction	Hartrigg moraine	Solifluction and nivation
		Giant deer	Detritus mud Windermere	Lunds organic deposits
		Solifluction	Nibthwaite & Haverthwaite moraines	
	Cranstal till (ablation till) Ballaquark till	Upper sands and gravels Upper till — Bride Moraine	Scottish Readvance	
18,990 BP Glen Ballyre gravels Kettle basin Orrisdale till gravels	Ballavarkish till 19,000-25,000 BP (Bride moraine) Shellag till — Kionlough till			
		Middle sands and gravels		
Mooar till (local) Ballateare till (foreign)	Head Ballure till (foreign)	Lower till	Main Lake District ice	Main Dales ice
	Rounded erratics in deposit on old beach platform	Point of Ayre Marine Interglacial deposits	Appleby ox tooth	
		Lowest sand and gravel		
		Lowest till	Maximum Lake District ice	Maximum Dales ice

Durham	Wear Lowland	East Durham Plateau	Tees Lowland	
(Smith & Francis 1967)		(Beaumont)		
	Terrace formation, stream incision	Cliff recession	Deposition in estuary, stream incision	Flandrian
				Zone III
		Zones I-III silts	III silts & clays	Zone II
			II Neasham peat	(Allerød)
			I silts & clays	Zone I
Upper till	Periglacial activity	Periglacial activity		Late Devensian
	Wear clay	Prismatic clay	Tees clays & sand	(Weichsel)
Upper middle sands				
		Moraine and Upper till	Upper till sand and gravel	26,000 BP
Easington raised beach	Laminated clay sand & gravel	Middle sands	Laminated clays	Middle
			Stainmore till	
Lower middle sands	Lower till	Lower till	Lower till	50,000 BP
Lower till				
(Easington raised beach)		? Easington raised beach — shells dated 38,000		Ipswichian (Eemian)
(Lower till)?		Scandinavian drift		Wolstonian (Saale)
		Warren House Gill till of western origin to provide erratics for raised beach		
Scandinavian drift				
				Hoxnian

Striding Edge. Many of the best-developed corries face east or north which is the direction in which snow drifts can accumulate and melting is reduced. Many of the corries are probably a late development in the landscape, having formed during one of the later phases of glaciation in Zones I and III.

The distribution of corries in terms of aspect, relief and altitude has been analysed by P.H. Temple (1965). The corrie groups analysed lie in the west central Lake District, between Cummock Water and Coniston. The aspect of the corries is predominantly northeast, this quadrant accounting for 52% of the total. The northwestern one has 23%, the southeastern 19% and the southwestern only 6%. There is no very marked pattern of elevation with respect to aspect, although the corries are lower in the marginal areas in response to the general land level. All the corries occur above 300 m. Climatic controls dominate the pattern, structure appearing to play a secondary role.

The more vigorous glaciers of the earlier phases of glaciation produced the glaciated valleys with their characteristic over-deepened, irregular, longitudinal profiles and hanging tributaries, the former resulting in the long lakes that give the district its name. Despite the generally glaciated appearance of the Lake District, the fact that preglacial erosion surfaces have been recognised throughout the area suggests that glacial erosion has been restricted to certain parts of the region, particularly to the valleys where the ice was flowing faster and was thicker. Much of the higher, flatter parts of the interfluves have probably been relatively little altered by glacial erosion. In the valleys on the other hand, active ice has been responsible for the formation of glacial diffluence and transfluence troughs, providing useful lines of communication, such as Dunmail Raise, eroded along a shatter belt, and the trough between St Bees and Whitehaven. Nowhere in the Lake District has the landscape been completely remodelled by ice action as it has in parts of northwest Scotland, although the details of the landscape are largely the result of glaciation. In the major troughs, such as the Windermere valley, there are well defined rock basins formed where additional ice reached the valley.

The northern basin of Windermere descends to -21 m OD

(Howell 1971) and is formed where the ice from Langdale met
that coming from the Ambleside direction. The Troutbeck valley,
which joins the basin a little further south, did not cause another
basin to form because the valley widens at this point so that over-
deepening did not take place at this junction. The northern rock
basin is separated from the southern part by a rock bar covered
nowhere by water deeper than 2.4 m. The drift floor of the
southern basin is at – 6.1 m OD with the lake surface at 66 m OD.
Howell has shown that sediment depths reach 21 m in the
northern basin and 40 m in the southern one. There are two distinct types of sediment, the lower sediments showing distortion
in places. The slopes of the basins slope steeply (up to 1 in 5 in
places) and the lake floor is irregular. The lack of erosion at the
site of the rock bar may have been due to the escape of ice eastwards down the Winster valley at this point. The depth of the
lake is increased by the presence of a terminal moraine at its
mouth, but it is nevertheless a true rock basin. Ice escaped by
various routes from the lake basin area; some passed eastwards
into the Kent valley via the Gowan where Staveley [470975]
now stands, some passed down the Winster valley from Bowness,
while at the southern end of the Lake ice moved both southeast
and southwest at different stages.

Coster and Gerrard (1947) have carried out a seismic refraction study of the outlet of Lake Windermere. The present lake
drains southwest through the narrow rock gorge of Backborrow
from Newby Bridge, while a wider valley lies open to the south-
south-east towards Cartmel. The seismic observations showed
that neither of these valleys has a thick covering of drift and at its
present level Windermere could not have drained out through the
open valley to Cartmel as there is a sill at Newby Bridge. The
only possible outlet up to 15 m above the present lake level is
through the present outlet via the Leven valley and Backborrow
gorge. Gresswell suggests that the present outlet of the lake was
first cut by melt-waters and then was followed by a small glacier
and it has been deepened 12 m by postglacial erosion, thus allowing the level of the lake to fall.

Isle of Man It is interesting to compare the effects of glacial erosion in the Lake District with those in the Isle of Man. The rocks of the Isle of Man are comparable with the slates of the Skiddaw area in the northern Lake District, so that this factor should not account for all the differences. In the Skiddaw slate area of the Lake District, although the glacial features are not quite so clearly marked as they are in the Borrowdale Volcanic area, there are several well developed corries on Saddleback [323277] and hanging valleys and other glacial forms also occur. In the hills of the Isle of Man, on the other hand, there is practically no evidence of glacial erosion with one important exception. The hills are smooth and there are no corries, although some periglacial forms exist which will be mentioned later.

The reason for this difference is that the hills of the Isle of Man have been uncovered by ice since the early ice advance, which took place during the Wolstonian period. There has, therefore, probably been a very long time interval during which the area has undergone non-glacial modification. This has produced the rounded and smooth outlines of the present relief. The Lake District on the other hand, contained active glaciers as recently as 10,000 BP and these recent glaciers were responsible for some of the obvious glacial forms. The milder, maritime climate of the Isle of Man and the lower elevation of the hills are responsible for the glacial contrasts in the two areas.

There is only one major glaciated valley in the Isle of Man, nearly all the others being youthful V-shaped fluvial valleys. The glaciated valley forms the main trough of low ground running between Douglas on the east and Peel on the west. This through trough has been cut by ice moving across a former water-parting running from Greeba Mountain [317916] on the north to Cregy Whuallian [313800] on the south. The ice formed a deep, U-shaped trough, causing the diversion of the upper Greeba river eastwards from its former westward course. The northeastern end of Slieau Whallian [265804] has been truncated by ice, which probably moved eastwards to cut this transfluent trough (see fig. 2.6 section AB).

Howgill Fells Another interesting contrast is found between the Lake District and the Howgill Fells to the east. Again rock conditions cannot account for all the differences in the features due to glacial erosion, because the Howgill Fells are composed of rocks similar to those of the southern Lake District in which glacial forms are present, although they are not quite so strikingly developed as in the Borrowdale Volcanic area. The reason for the relatively small amount of glacial erosion in the Howgill Fells was due to the relative slow velocity of the ice, which was not free to move unimpeded from the Howgill Fells owing to the Lake District and Pennine ice hemming it in on either side. The local ice-cap of the Howgill Fells was also probably relatively thin because this area lies at a lower elevation than the Lake District and is partially in its rain shadow and, therefore, receives less precipitation, amounting to a little over 1800 mm/yr. Oughtershaw Hall [873811], which is a little further east, receives 1625 mm/yr.

The rounded summits of the Howgill Fells are almost devoid of the forms of glacial erosion. Cautley Crags [680970] are the only conspicuous feature of glacial erosion. The crags surround a rather poorly developed corrie that faces northeast above the Rawthey valley. This corrie backwall is of interest because it has cut back through a valley side to cause the diversion of Red Gill Beck, the former head of the Lune, to the Rawthey. This captured stream now falls over Cautley Spout in a 180 m high series of waterfalls to join the Rawthey. Somewhat similar poorly developed corries occur in the Lune Gorge [607998], where they also face eastwards. The Lune gorge itself suggests glacial overdeepening by ice passing through from the north, a direction supported by the presence of Shap granite erratics in the gorge. The cutting of the gorge by an early diffluent glacier has already been suggested as a possibility. This must have occurred before the knick-point moved upstream to Tebay.

Cheviot Hills Glacial erosion in the Cheviot Hills and Pennines is limited for the same reasons as it is in the Howgill Fells. The Cheviots did not form their own ice-cap (Common 1954) and the hill summits were not covered by the maximum ice advances. On the east side of the hills the ice reached an elevation of 520 to 530 m during the maximum advance, but the period of covering by ice above 300 m was probably fairly short. Features of ice erosion are, therefore, only of a minor nature. Their distribution suggests that the ice of the upper layers moved in a different direction to the ice in the lower levels, which was constrained by valleys.

On the lower ground closer to the sea the ice moving south scoured the exposed harder bands, such as the Whin Sill, especially where these lay athwart the direction of ice movement. Where the sandstone scarps lay parallel to the ice flow their form was merely accentuated. Common does not consider that there are any corries on the Cheviots. Features that have been taken for corries are more likely to be the result of nivation and will be mentioned later in connection with periglacial activity.

C.M. Clapperton (1970) has re-examined the evidence for glacial erosion on the Cheviots. The Cheviot Massif rises to 816 m in the igneous area east of the Silurian and Carboniferous hills. Glacial action is less evident on the higher hills than it is below 300 m. Various opinions concerning ice accumulation on the Cheviots have been expressed. Clough considered that the Cheviot was an independent ice centre, but Carruthers, Common and Sissons considered that the area was not a centre of ice dispersal, and the latter considered that it had not even been ice-covered. Erratics are found to a height of 580 m. Evidence of striations suggests diverging glacier ice from the present watershed in the central Cheviots. Ice flowed northeast down Teviotdale on the northern flanks of the hills, while an ice sheet moving east by north from the Tyne gap affected the southern flanks. There is no evidence of glaciation on the igneous massif itself, and no erratics have been discovered above 300 m, although they are abundant at lower levels. Igneous erratics occur in the eastern drift, but they extend no further west than Redesdale and are not common in Lower Redesdale. Clapperton concludes that local ice probably occupied upper Redesdale and prevented over-riding of ice coming from the west via the Solway and Tweed valleys. The presence of granite erratics on andesite at 580 m show that ice moved south-south-east from the centre of the Cheviot massif. Till composed only of igneous rocks in Lambden, Harthope and Shank Burne and the river Breamish valley also indicate locally generated ice. Meltwater channels are concentrated below 365 m in the western extremity of the massif. They are more numerous in the east than the west. The central ice mass probably did not extend beyond Ingram in the Breamish valley. The lack of channels in the west is due to water flowing down pre-existing valleys. The channels in the northern, northeastern, and southern and southeastern, parts of the area are related to invading ice masses.

Erosional activity is indicated in the Bizzle amphitheatre, which has a cirque form. Hen Hole and other cirques also occur. Ice erosion may have been responsible for the valley asymmetry, as suggested by the occurrence of roches moutonnées. Glaciers flowing north were diverted west from the Bizzle-Bellyside area. Evidence of ice erosion in College valley also requires local, rather than invading, ice. Bizzle cirque contains deposits that Clapperton interpreted as moraine, probably of lateglacial date and found at 395 to 455 m. Similar deposits in College valley merge downstream into steeply sloping outwash. If ice could form moraines in the lateglacial, it must have been more extensive at the maximum of the Devensian. Deeply-rotted rock lies above the level of subglacial meltwater channels and is overlain by till. It is, therefore, not evidence of an unglaciated enclave. Tors occur at 395 and 660 m, the best examples of which are Standrop Tors at 525 and 530 m. Others show possible glacial streamlining in the Harthope valley at 395 m. The tors can apparently survive relatively slow-moving ice better than severe periglacial processes. The local and foreign ice masses became confluent at their maximum extent.

Pennines The Alston block presents a high and continuous face to the west so that heavy snow-falls could be expected in this vicinity during glacial phases. Thus it is not surprising that this high ground nourished its own ice cap and that glaciers moving down from this gathering ground to the west, with a steep gradient, were able to produce some U-shaped valleys and corries, as noted by Trotter (1929b). The thickness of the ice was such that, as in the Cheviots, the upper ice moved in general eastwards with the slope of the ice surface, while the lower ice moved down the valleys, constrained by the relief. Trotter has shown that ice from the Lake District and Scotland must have been powerful in the northern part of the Pennine escarpment and erratics from these areas have been carried up to 590 m O.D. along and across the escarpment. This ice was part of the stream that passed east across the Tyne Gap. To the south the local ice was powerful enough to keep off the ice coming from distant sources.

In the Askrigg block ice was local in origin and ice erosion was strongly localised. There is considerably more ground above 600 m at the head of the Ure and Eden valleys around Baugh Fell and Wild Boar Fell than there is in the Lake District, and this high area provided a powerful source of ice that moved down all the valleys in the district. The ice did not produce much over-deepening, but was probably responsible for the formation of the limestone scars that are so characteristic of the Dales, by scouring off the weathered mantle. The congestion of ice to the south of the dales prevented much over-deepening by the generally slow-moving ice.

However, in some dales the local relief enabled more effective glacial erosion to take place and U-shaped valleys were formed. The two best examples are upper Wharfedale and Bishopdale. These valleys are so situated that they received a large volume of ice moving east from Langstrothdale Chase as it impinged onto Buckden Pike (see fig. 4.7). This high ground diverted the ice to south and north to flow respectively down upper Wharfedale and Bishopdale. The ice in the latter valley had a steep gradient at the valley head, and was able to scour the valley bottom to such an extent that the main valley now hangs to its short tributary, Bishopdale, at their confluence just below the Aysgarth Falls. The presumed knick-point in the Bishopdale valley has been removed by glacial erosion (King 1936). Bishopdale thus forms a strong contrast to its southern neighbour Walden, which was protected from the ice by the bulk of Buckden Pike, and which is now a V-shaped valley, showing very little sign of glacial erosion. Their contrasting cross profiles are shown in fig. 4.3. Littondale is another valley the situation of which has allowed it to become scoured by ice and it now has a wide flat floor. K.M. Clayton (1966) has suggested that Snaizeholme [835850] to the west of

Dodd Fell is an example of an intrusive trough, having been shaped by ice moving southwest from the high ground above Hawes towards Ribblehead, where drumlin alignment indicates ice flow south down Ribblesdale and southwest along the Greta valley. The ice could have come from Shunner Fell, Baugh Fell and the Widdale Fell area of accumulation at the head of Wensleydale. Clayton also draws attention to the effective glacial erosion in the valleys on either side of Penyghent, where a series of five glacial troughs sweep round from west to south to join the Ribble valley. The troughs also contain aligned drumlins.

Lancashire lowlands The effects of glacial erosion on the Lancashire Plain are by no means as obvious as those in the highland part of Northern England. Nevertheless, as shown by Gresswell (1964) probably some of the most spectacular glacial erosion in the whole area took place in this area, although the evidence is now mainly hidden underground. Gresswell has shown how the Mersey and Dee estuaries have been influenced by glacial erosion as well as other parallel valleys in the area around Liverpool. The Dee estuary has parallel sides, about four miles apart, while the Mersey has a narrow entrance and widens out southeast of Liver-

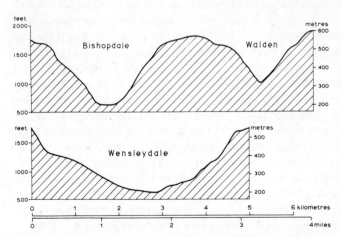

Fig. 4.3 The contrasting profiles of Bishopdale and Walden and Wensleydale in the Askrigg block. (See figure 4.7 for the position of the profiles.)

pool around Ellesmere Port. The narrows are partly due to the
outcrop of harder rocks between Liverpool and Bootle on the
east and Birkenhead and Wallasey on the west. The ground rises
rapidly to 60 m either side of the narrows within a mile of the
coast, although further inland the ground is much lower even
further from the margin of the inner estuary. Two further depressions lie parallel to these two major estuaries. These are the
mid-Wirral depression, which runs from Leasowe [270907] to
Hooton [350782], and the Alt Ditton depression, in which the
river Alt flows northwest between Kirkby and Maghull on the
east and Liverpool on the west.

All these depressions run from north-north-west to south-
south-east, and they are termed iceways by Gresswell. He suggests
that they were eroded by concentrated streams of Irish Sea ice as
the ice-sheet was constrained to flow through a narrow gap
between the Pennines on the east and the Welsh uplands on the
west, as it flowed towards the Shropshire-Cheshire plain to the
south. The pattern of the iceways is shown in fig. 4.4. The four
major ice-eroded channels are linked in places by cross channels.
One of these is the Float iceway [300910], which links the northern end of the Mid-Wirral iceway with the Mersey iceway
between Wallasey and Birkenhead. The ice from the Alt Ditton
iceway escaped further south by way of the Weaver iceway and
the Peckmill iceway. In this area the ice came up against the high
ground near Frodsham [517767] which reaches an altitude of
146 m. About a mile away to the north the greatest erosion
depth is found near Frodsham Bridge, where the rock beneath the
drift is at −72 m, giving a height range of more than 200 m over a
short distance. All the iceways show irregular glacial scouring.
Depths reach −46 m at the entrance to the Float iceway on Wirral
and −55 m at the northern end of the mid-Wirral iceway. The Dee
iceway has been eroded to depths in excess of 80 m below sea-
level in several areas, and all the other iceways have hollows extending well below the present sea-level. The hollows could have
been cut either by the ice itself or by subglacial melt-waters. The
latter seems more likely in view of the close proximity of the
channels and the depth of the basins. The ice that eroded these
channels was forced into the narrow 40 km gap between the hills

as it escaped from the very congested piedmont lobe in the Irish Sea. The channels are somewhat similar to the transgressive troughs discussed by Linton (1957), in that the ice was forced to flow from a lower and wider area through a relatively narrow gap; they might also be classified as intrusive troughs. This appears to be the only place where the relief was such that deep channels could be eroded by ice in this way. The deep holes occur where the constriction was greatest, such as near Frodsham. The Dee was the largest of the iceways. They are all typical of erosion by slowly moving ice over friable bedrock.

P.T. Howell (1973) has discussed the subdrift surface of the Mersey and Weaver catchment and adjacent area. The surface is defined by contouring from 1450 boreholes and a coastal seismic

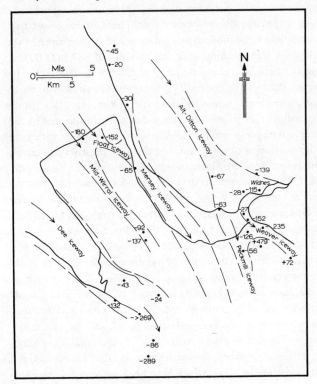

Fig. 4.4 The iceways of south Lancashire (After R.K. Gresswell.)

profile series. The subdrift surface is dissected by Gresswell's ice-ways; however, Howell is of the opinion that the orientation and pattern of the valleys is more consistent with a view that they are subaerial fluvial valleys, modified by glacial meltwaters under hydrostatic pressure, to form the closed depression along their courses. The valley form suggests rejuvenation related to low sea-levels, as in places they are below the present Ordnance Datum level. One difficulty in the interpretation is the possible error in some of the data, due to subsidence, problems of interpreting the type of material and other uncertainties.

Many of the valleys have a southeast to northwest trend, such as those running through the sites of Wigan, Upholland, Liverpool and the Weaver valley. Much of the Lancashire plain sub-drift surface is below 30 m, and 77,700 ha are below present sea level in the Lancashire-Cheshire area. There are major subdrift valleys below the modern Dee, Mersey and Weaver rivers, that below the Dee reaching a maximum depth of −87 m O.D. in an ungraded course. An isolated hollow 6 km wide and 10 km long, deeper than −30 m occurs. The Mersey valley runs from northeast to southwest across the base of the Wirral to link with the Dee valley; this valley is also ungraded and runs normal to the direction of presumed ice flow. Many of the smaller valleys runs from northwest to southeast, but they are mostly very narrow. The valleys tend to widen and deepen towards the major valleys and the sea. The present drainage follows the subdrift valley system, which as a whole was probably initiated in the Tertiary or Quaternary. The shape and pattern of the valleys does not support a glacial origin, because their direction is not related to ice flow patterns. Their ungraded long profiles present problems, as rock barriers occur about 30 m below sea level. Some hollows are the result of salt subsidence, for example at Northwich, and some, such as those near Chester, may be the result of glacial abrasion. However, most closed depressions occur within the valley system on the Permo-Triassic rocks, and they are most likely to be due to glacial meltwater confined under pressure beneath the ice sheet, causing local scouring. They would, therefore, be tunnel valleys, which have been preserved by burial under drift, deposited soon after their formation. Thus many of

the valleys combine preglacial and glacial elements, and they
show evidence of varying base-levels in their rejuvenation. The
valley pattern is shown in fig. 4.5.

Glacial deposition

The main areas of glacial deposition are the lowlands and the
valleys within the highlands. The northern part of the Isle of
Man is characterised by very thick glacial deposits with their base
well below sea-level. Elsewhere the drift cover is thinner, although it is still significant in forming the details of the landscape. Glacial deposits vary according to the character of the till
of which they are composed, the movement of the ice, and the
age of the deposit.

In some areas the deposits are found as valley fills without
distinctive form. In County Durham drift fills deep buried valleys,
while in other areas drumlins or drift tails give a distinctive
character to the landscape, and halt stages during retreat can be

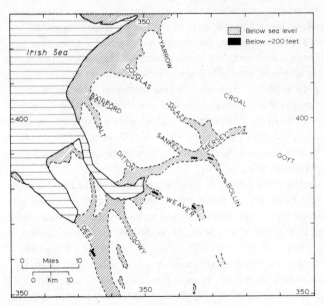

Fig. 4.5 The sub-drift surface, showing buried valleys, in the south Lancashire area. (After F.T. Howell.)

identified by end moraine deposits. These will be considered last as in some instances they merge into the glacifluvial deposits to be considered in the next section.

The erratic content of the drifts is of great value in assessing the direction of movement and source of the ice, and several valuable marker rocks are found in Northern England. The Shap granite is one of the best known and easily identified and gives valuable evidence of the dispersal of ice from the southeastern Lake District. Its distribution suggests that the basal ice and the upper layers often moved in different directions, as pointed out by Hollingworth (1931) and shown in the inset of figure 4.1. The igneous rocks of the Lake District and Cheviots also provide useful marker erratics. Much of the till of the district is true boulder clay, consisting of fairly large, often striated boulders set in a fine clayey matrix. This material is well exposed in many of the valleys within the area, the boulder content and matrix type varying from place to place.

One of the areas where the valleys are filled with a thick layer of drift is in the highland part of the Isle of Man. In Druidale [370880], for example, the stream has exposed a 22 m high section in a very bouldery deposit but the deposit has little superficial expression merely filling the valley floor. At present it is being dissected by the stream. There was some evidence that some of the material may have slumped into the valley subsequent to its original deposition, and its formless surface character is probably due to the long period since this part of the island was covered by moving ice. The problem is further discussed in the periglacial section.

Another area where the valleys tend to be choked by till is the Howgill Fells. The ice was slow moving on account of its inability to escape freely and thus deposited its locally derived load in the valley bottom. It is now being excavated by the stream, producing in places high till cliffs along the streams and a type of bad-land relief in some valleys, for example a northern tributary of Carlin Gill [628000]. Thus in these two widely separated areas valleys are choked by drift in a similar way but for different reasons.

As in the Howgill Fells and Isle of Man upland valleys, the till of the Cheviots appears to contain largely local material. It has been shown by Clapperton that Cheviot ice was generated locally, so the drift consists of local material. A period of deep weathering preceded the last glaciation in the Cheviot region, thus providing local material that the glaciers could rework and deposit as till. The same argument would also help to account for the thick drift of local material that was deposited in the Howgill and Manx valleys, and in many of the Pennine valleys of the Askrigg block.

The matrix of the till over much of the area reflects the character of the weak bands within the strata, thus it is composed largely of shale in the Pennines and eastern part of the region, where this material is abundant in the Carboniferous rocks. The New Red sandstone outcrops frequently provide a reddish matrix, for example in the tills of part of the Eden valley. Relatively smooth and featureless expanses of till are rare, apart from the instances cited. This is in part a reflection of the recent date of much of the glacial deposition in this area, allowing the original forms of deposition to survive.

D. Huddart (1971) has shown that the sand/matrix ratio provides a method of correlating till units in the Cumberland lowland. The matrix is defined as the silt + clay. This ratio allows Main Glaciation tills to be differentiated from those of the Scottish Readvance. The recorded values are as follows:

| | Edenside and Carlisle Plain | | West and South Cumberland | |
	Main Glac.	Scots. Readv.	Main Glac.	Scots. Readv.
Mean	0.62	0.29	0.57	0.22
Standard deviation	0.195	0.15	0.20	0.09

The t-test gave a t value of 6.59, significant at the 99% level. The Scottish Readvance till is much finer, due to the reworking of older tills, and the incorporation of its own outwash, including proglacial lake deposits. The main glacial till contains much local bedrock.

P.F. Worthington (1972) has discussed a resistivity survey of the drift deposits of part of the Fylde area. The drift deposits reach a thickness of 45 m, and consist largely of till with some sand and gravel. The surface is pitted by kettle holes. The till overlies a bedrock of mainly Bunter in the area studied, which covered 43 km^2 in the Wyre valley east of Fleetwood and north-west of Preston. It includes the confluences of the rivers Calder and Brock with the Wyre. A buried channel in bedrock underlies the present Wyre valley. The drift is all till in the west, but in places it is underlain by sands and gravel especially in the north-east, where the stratified deposits are underlain by a lower till, while in places upper sands and gravel overlie the main till, thus giving four divisions. All four belong to the Newer Drift division. Drift thicknesses mostly lie between 10 and 30 m, but are thicker in the buried valleys.

The orientation and type of stones in the Lower till sheet of eastern Durham are discussed by P. Beaumont (1971). The results show an ice movement from west-north-west to east-south-east. Ice in the area came from Scandinavia, the Lake District, the Pennines and the Cheviot Hills. Three till sheets have been recognised, the oldest being the Scandinavian drift in Warren House Gill, and this is overlain by the most widespread till sheet of eastern Durham, the Lower till. It rests on bedrock and is 6 to 9 m thick in many places, and is very compacted. The Upper till forms a belt 1 to 14 km wide in the coastal zone only. It has fewer stones and is less compacted than the Lower till. The 180 degree orientation analysis showed a preferred orientation to the southeast on the east Durham plateau from Seaham to Newton Aycliffe. Near the coast between Seaham and West Hartlepool the orientation suggests onshore movement with north-north-east to north-north-west directions of flow. Igneous rocks in the till are derived mainly from the Cheviots to the north and the Lake District to the west and the Whin Sill dolerites and basalts. Nearer east Durham the ice must have crossed sedimentary Carboniferous rocks, including grits, lime-stone and Coal Measures, and nearer still it crossed the Mag-nesian limestone outcrop. The till on the plateau east of the Magnesian limestone scarp has the most mixed assemblage of stones, including Magnesian limestone up to 20%, while it con-stitutes 44% of the Lower till of the coastal region. Trend surface analysis was used to study the distribution of erratics of different types, although levels of explanation were on the whole low, only reaching 43% for the first degree surface for Magnesian limestone, 41% for the first degree surface for sandstone and 31% for coal, siltstone and ironstone. The trends confirm an ice movement towards the east-south-east. Both Upper and Lower tills are probably of Devensian age.

J.T. Andrews and D. Ingle Smith (1970) discuss till fabrics recorded in cliff sections along the Yorkshire coast from Robin Hood's Bay to Runswick Bay, including sites near Whitby and Upgang. At Upgang the glacial deposits are complex and include current bedded sands, till and varves, and at Whitby there are bedded sands within the till. Glacial deposits are well exposed in Robin Hoods' Bay, where till sections reach heights of 40 m in places, and are more uniform than at the other sites. The bedrock-till junction is also well exposed and often complex, including varved and laminated sediments and a sandstone pavement. The results of a detailed analysis of the fabrics measured show that there is a difference between those in Robin Hood's Bay and those recorded elsewhere. In Robin Hood's Bay the mean orientations are predominantly east-west, and nearly all mean dips are down to the east, while in all the other areas the mean orientations are predominantly north-south with dips more equally divided, although most are southwards. A possible explanation is that fabrics are transverse in Robin Hood's Bay, owing to ascending ice flow up a bedrock slope, on the other hand the data could be interpreted as an early movement from the east and later movement from the north. The Robin Hood's Bay group have low dips, strong secondary maxima, 93.5% dip east, and there is high clustering about the mean. The results are not easy to interpret in terms of ice movement in this area, and provide a warning against too ready conclusions concerning ice flow from the study of till fabrics, which are often extremely complex and variable.

Drumlins and drift-tails One of the most conspicuous and widespread forms in which glacial till has been deposited in northern England is as drumlins. These are abundant in many parts of the region but are restricted to the lower ground, only rarely occurring above 300 m. Drumlins are of considerable interest both for the light they throw on the mechanism of glacial movement and for the information they give of former directions of ice movement.

The main drumlin fields in Northern England are found in the extreme north, in the lowland area just south of the lower Tweed in Northumberland. The Lake District is almost entirely surrounded by drumlins. The drumlin field to the north in the Solway lowlands continues eastwards through the Tyne gap almost to the east coast and the Eden valley is full of drumlins, which also extend up towards the Stainmore gap. Drumlins occur widely to the southeast of the Lake District around Kendal and spread into the area between the Ribble and Aire south of Settle. They are found in the upper Ribble valley and at the head of the Ure and Eden and extend in ones and twos into all the major valleys and also occur in the south of the Isle of Man (see fig. 4.6). The distribution of drumlins, which often lie at the foot of the steeper slopes and on cols and divides, suggests that they tend to occur in those areas where the movement of the ice was constrained, partly by reduction of gradient and partly as a result of interference by other ice masses or glacial diffluence.

The drumlins of the Eden valley area may be taken as an example for more detailed consideration and are shown on fig. 4.6. These drumlins have been studied by Hollingworth (1931) and they illustrate many points of interest. The elongation, or length to breadth ratio, of the drumlins varies from 1-1 to 1-6, and it is suggested that this variation depends partly on the speed and constancy of direction of ice flow. Where the ice was moving fast and uniformly the elongation of the drumlin is greater, but where the ice was congested and moving more erratically the drumlins become almost circular or irregular.

In this area also it is possible to demonstrate that the drumlins cannot have been formed submarginally. The pattern of the drumlins in the Eden valley is such that their elongation near Shap is north-south, at Penrith they have changed to north-north-west to south-south-east, further north near Rosley [320453] they are aligned northwest to southeast, swinging round to west-east near Wigton and southwest to northeast near Aspatria. This

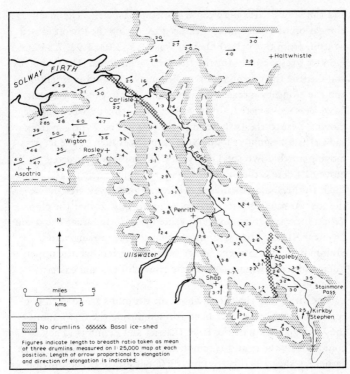

Fig. 4.6 The distribution, orientation and elongation of the drumlins in the Eden valley.

pattern demonstrates that a fast-flowing and powerful stream of Lake District ice, flowing down the Eden valley, was diverted west and southwest by ice from Scotland, a situation that must have existed during the maximum of the glaciation. During the retreat phases, when the ice margin was in the vicinity of Wigton the ice from the Lake District would have parted from the Scottish ice and be moving from south to north, at right angles to the trend of the drumlins.

The figures and arrows on the map (fig. 4.6) indicate the elongation of the drumlins and the orientation of their long axes. It can be shown statistically that there is a significant difference in elongation between the drumlins of the area near Appleby, the Eden valley a little further north, the Carlisle area, the Tyne gap and the Solway area between Wigton and Aspatria. The mean elongation of 20 drumlins measured by taking the lowest closed contour from the 1:25,000 maps was 2.55, 3.03, 1.92, 2.85 and 4.66 to 1 respectively for the five areas mentioned. Near Appleby and Carlisle the drumlin pattern becomes confused in orientation and the elongation reaches a minimum. It is in these areas that basal ice-sheds existed, forming lines of parting between the ice moving west to the Irish Sea and east across the Tyne gap from the Carlisle neighbourhood. Near Appleby, much of the ice was moving north down the Eden valley but some was diverted to move east across the Stainmore gap, forming another basal ice-shed. In the Tyne gap and especially in the Solway area, however, the ice was moving faster and more uniformly so that the elongation increases to a maximum value in the latter area. The drumlins near Kirkby Stephen indicate that the ice moving across Stainmore was reinforced by ice moving north down the upper Eden and ice moving out from the Howgill Fells and eastern Lake District.

The erratics in the till of which the drumlins are formed confirms that they must have been formed during the maximum of the Main glaciation of the Lake District and Pennines. They could not be the result of remodelling of the till deposited by an earlier ice-sheet, as this contains different erratics. The distribution of erratics in the drumlins and in drifts further afield shows that the basal ice-sheds which determined the orientation of the drumlins did not coincide with the upper ice-sheds indicating that there must have been differential movement within the ice. Thus although the basal ice moved north continuously from the Shap area, as indicated by drumlin alignment, few granite erratics from Shap are found north of the mouth of Ullswater. They must mostly have been carried up into the upper layers of ice that were moving eastwards across Stainmore from this position, following the general slope of the ice surface as shown in the inset in fig. 4.1. This was possibly due to the effect of a powerful glacier moving down Ullswater.

In Wensleydale the drumlins along the valley sides have amalgamated to form drumlinoid drift-tails which have had a marked effect on the drainage pattern (see fig. 4.7). The con-

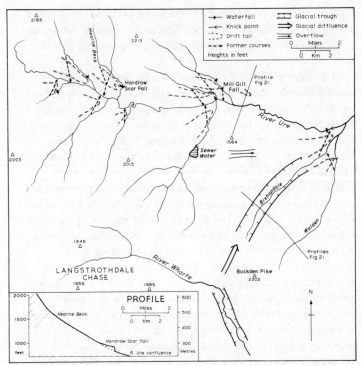

Fig. 4.7 The drift-tails of Wensleydale and the drainage modifications to which they have given rise.

siderable amount of glacial deposition in this valley is probably due to the blocking of the lower end of the valley by the main Vale of York glacier, which would prevent the Wensleydale glacier from flowing freely and fast. The drift-tails are plastered along the valley sides by the ice so that the spurs of tributary dales are elongated down valley and their streams have been pushed eastwards. This frequently has the effect of modifying their stream profiles, making them flatter than formerly as they flow behind the drift tail, but they often fall to the main valley over a waterfall as they flow round the end of the drift tail. Many of the falls in the tributary valleys of Wensleydale are of this type, for example Hardrow Scar [869917] fall, Mill Gill Force [939914] and Whitfield Gill Force [935923]. These features are best developed in Wensleydale as this valley is wider than many of the other Pennine Dales, and it also receives many tributary valleys, the streams of which can be diverted in this way.

A detailed study of the till fabric in one isolated valley bottom drumlin shows that the orientations of the preferred vector of long axes vary with elevation and position in the drumlin. There is a tendency for the preferred vector to turn increasingly in towards the centre line of the drumlin. The mean of all vectors for ten samples of 50 stones each made an angle of $20°$ with the drumlin elongation. These observations suggest that till was plastered onto a growing accumulation by a lateral pressure in the ice. This drumlin consists mainly of till, which is 46% sand, 30% silt, and 24% clay. There are also small patches of stratified material at the proximal or stoss end of the drumlin, indicating some water-deposited material, (Andrews and King 1968).

Moraines As drumlins give evidence of the direction and character of ice flow during the glacial maxima, so moraines are valuable in providing information concerning the stages of retreat of the ice, as they form during minor still stands or advances in a period of general retreat and deglaciation. Most of the conspicuous moraines in the region are found in the valleys. They mostly formed when the ice-sheets had shrunk to valley glaciers and were retreating back into the mountains.

An exception is the moraine that must have formed marginally to the ice-sheet that spread westwards into eastern County Durham to deposit the upper till. This ice formed a north-south belt of moraine during a slight halt or readvance lying a few miles inland. The Isle of Man has no moraines of the valley glacier type, although it has a very large ice-sheet moraine the Bride moraine which has already been mentioned. The valley glacier type of moraine is formed of unsorted till, often rather more gravelly than the drumlin till, because much of the finer material has been washed away by meltwater.

The valleys of the Yorkshire Pennines show the pattern of terminal moraines particularly clearly, and they have been described by Raistrick (1927) who has mapped them in each major valley.

He has found evidence for six halt stages in the valleys of the
Aire and Wharfe, but not all these stages are seen in the northern
valleys, the Nidd, Ure and Swale (see fig. 2.8) owing to later
separation from the Vale of York glacier. Many of these moraines, which appear to be very recent because of their fresh,
hummocky character, dammed up elongated lakes in the valley
upstream. Some of the lakes in Airedale must have been nearly
30 m deep. These have since been filled with laminated clays and
fine silts to form flat, frequently flooded, sections of the valley
floor. The moraines of the Wharfe valley are situated at Pool (1),
Burley (2), Middleton (3), Drebley (4), Kilnsey (5) and Skirfare
Bridge (6), in order up valley. The Skirfare Bridge moraine in the
Wharfe has been correlated with one at Cononley (6) in the Aire,
at Hawes (6) on the Ure and Gunnerside (6) on the Swale.

Still more recent moraines are found in the Lake District as
the valley glaciers retreated back into the hills, the last of all
being the small corrie moraines formed by the glaciers that
formed in Zone III. True moraines of this recent date are probably restricted in Northern England to the Lake District, as it
was only here that genuine glaciers formed at this time, with the
possible exception of the highest hills around Cross Fell.
Manley's (1959) evidence on this point has been cited already.

During the post-Allerød cold phase in Zone III, valley glaciers
in the Lake District descended to 140-150 m in Wastdale, Langdale and Borrowdale, 210 m in Grisedale, southeast of Helvellyn
and Easedale, 270 m in Ennerdale and 350 m in Eskdale (G.
Manley 1959). The deposits are those of relatively thin, stagnating glaciers that descended lower in the wetter, more shaded
valleys. At the same time tarn moraines, were being formed by
the more active ice in the corries at heights between 240 m and
700 m with a mean elevation of 490 m. These moraines indicate
the presence of active ice, especially in the deeper corrie basins
after the supply to the valley glaciers had been cut off and they
had become stagnant.

Moraine-like deposits in the Mallerstang area do not descend
below 380 m. Similar deposits occur at 525 m at Combe Bottom
[707838] south of Dent, and 590 m east of Whernside [742820].
In the Howgill Fells conditions are particularly favourable for

corrie ice formation in Cautley Crags, and ice descended to 430 m. The Pennines and Howgills were in a very marginal situation for corrie glacier formation at this time, and many of the features formed in these areas can probably best be accounted for by snow patch activity.

Glacifluvial features

Moraines of the type described in the Dales can only form where the ice is retreating upstream so that drainage is not impounded. In some parts of the area, for example the Cheviots and the western parts of the Alston block the ice retreated downslope away from the hills and the ice front frequently terminated in water. Under such conditions the retreat deposits are often stratified and the resulting features are glacifluvial forms.

Isle of Man The term 'delta-moraine' is a useful one for frontal features deposited by melt water into still water impounded in front of the ice. The largest moraine of this type is probably the Bride moraine in the north of the Isle of Man. This feature, which reaches a height of over 90 m above the surrounding low country, is very hummocky and fresh-looking. Although it contains some true till it consists largely of stratified sand, gravel and clay. The coarse morainic material including some shell fragments, showing that the ice depositing it came from the sea to the north, lies near the top of the section at Shellag Point [461998]. This suggests that the ice over-rode the deposits laid down in a proglacial lake, probably held up between the ice and the high ground to the south.

Slater (1931) described the Bride moraine in detail from Point Cranstal northwards, thus continuing the section already commented upon (p. 89). He considers that the stratigraphy consists of three main units. The lowest unit consists of silty clay in seams or lenses interbedded with sand and gravel, the middle series are clayey sands, occurring as three mounds, and the top sequence is a clayey, sandy till mixed with pebbles and boulders. The beds are contorted near Point Cranstal and thrust movement is suggested. He thought that these deposits were laid down by the gradual melting of a stagnant glacier, the deposits represent-

ing the gradual build up of ground moraine. He agrees with
Thomas (1971) that the ice only reached the position of the
higher part of the moraine and the southern sediments were
deposited proglacially, while the gradual melting away of the
stagnant ice in situ built up the northern part of the series.

The moraine marks the limit of ice advancing south down the
Irish Sea and stretches right across the north of the island. On the
west of the island near Orrisdale, there is also evidence of deltaic
formation in stratified sand dipping southwest. This was probably
laid down in water impounded between the ice to the north and
the high ground to the south at the same time as the Bride
moraine was accumulating in the east.

Glacifluvial sands and gravels are widespread in several parts of
Northern England. Considerable patches of sand and gravel

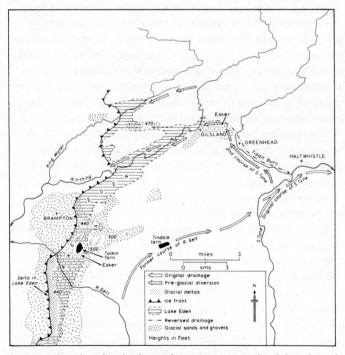

Fig. 4.8 Lake Eden, showing its maximum extent, associated deposits and
the drainage changes. (Based largely on the work of F.M. Trotter.)

occur, with undulating relief, on the eastern and northern sides of the Cheviot Hills, in some instances as at Bradford, Wark and Pallinsburn forming kames. These were laid down when the ice was retreating northwards away from the hills.

Alston block and Eden valley Another area where there is much glacifluvial material is around the northwestern margin of the Alston block where it has been studied by Trotter (1929). This was deposited as the Scottish and Lake District ice retreated downslope from the high ground, impounding a series of lakes as the level fell back (see fig. 4.8). An example of the type of feature that was formed is seen near Talkin Tarn [545590] south-east of Brampton. The tarn is held up between two eskers and two kames. Other features that are conspicuous in this area are deltas in glacial lakes. These features indicate the level of the lake and are useful in defining the retreat phases. Many of the deltas have steep ice-contact slopes at the rear formed by slump-ing as the ice melted away. A good example of an esker is found in the Tyne valley extending from Hexham to Haltwhistle, this was formed as the ice retreated upstream, but beyond the latter point the ice started to retreat downstream and a lake was held up, in which deltas and lake sediments accumulated.

This lake has been called Lake Eden and at its earliest stage it stood at 143 m O.D. as indicated by the height of the delta formed in it. The formation and development of this lake will be taken as an example of one of the major glacial diversions of drainage in the area, (see fig. 4.2). The lake was held up between the Scottish and Lake District ice, then in contact in the west, and the col that then existed between the South Tyne, which had drained west up to this time, and the West Allen draining east. The col was situated near Haltwhistle at 143 m, but it was lowered by the direct overflow from Lake Eden to 134 m and retreated west to near Greenhead, east of Gilsland. The outflow was lowered sufficiently by this stage to allow the South Tyne to be diverted eastwards when Lake Eden was drained. Evidence for the lake is seen in varied clays, and deposits of fine sand. In the process of diversion of the South Tyne the direction of drainage between Greenhead and Gilsland was reversed to flow east. When the two ice sheets parted the lake escaped westwards.

Another interesting drainage diversion caused by the action of meltwaters took place nearer the head of the Eden valley. As the ice retreated westwards towards the Lake District from Ash Fell Edge [735048] water was impounded between this high ground and the retreating ice to the west. Meltwaters escaped north-wards, crossing a col left dry by capture at 270 m and were able to cut down the level deeply enough to divert the stream once more to the Eden drainage, forming the 75 m deep Scandal Beck gorge [727070] , (see fig. 2.2). A little further west the deserted from the retreating Lake District ice. In producing these stream diversions the meltwaters accomplished considerable erosion.

Cheviot Hills A study of the Cheviot meltwater channels by Common (1957) gives some indication of the variety of features that occur in this area and their significance as indicators of glacial retreat (see fig. 4.9). Drainage channels are common in Cheviot partly because far travelled ice retreated towards the surrounding low ground, thus giving conditions in which drainage was ponded around or flowed in under the ice margin. The channels tend to form series running around the former margins of the ice lobes, but at times the water drained beneath the ice to form steeper subglacial chutes. In the area to the west and southwest of Wooler the following types of channels can be distinguished: (a) there are direct overflow channels cutting across the main watershed, for example Kingston Dean: (b) severed spurs form a second type and are frequently well marked features, such as south of Akeld: (c) marginal channels form a third type, these have only one side and are found round the north face of Humbledon Hill. The severed spur channels are usually cut through rock and may be 15 m to 45 m deep. The evidence is not sufficient to suggest that high level proglacial lakes existed in the area, although there may well have been low level lakes of small dimensions in the College and Bowmont valleys, and larger low-level lakes more certainly existed in other basins, such as the Aln, Hedgely and Milfield valleys. Although the individual channels vary, their position and characteristics enable them to be classified.

C. Clapperton (1966) has drawn attention in the Cheviot area
to the importance of the letting down of supra- and englacial
channels to form subglacial ones. This process would account for
channels that apparently bear little relation to the relief. On the
whole, however, in the east Cheviot area the major channels do
follow cols and valley heads. Complex anastomosing channels, up
to 18 m deep, occur 3 km west-south-west of Wooler, cut into a
broad col and wide valley. The concentration of water to cut
deep channels across cols and valley heads may be the result of
downslope migration. In more open ground more complex systems could become superimposed onto the ground from a supra-
or englacial position.

The deglaciation of the Cheviot Hills has been considered by
C.M. Clapperton (1971), who has identified four phases, (a) a
period of ice-directed meltwater drainage, (b) a period when the

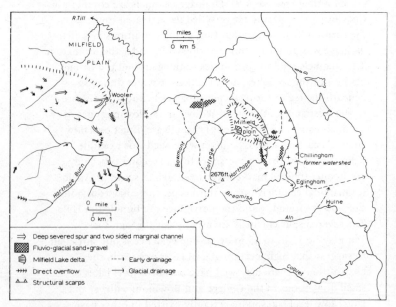

Fig. 4.9 Some features of the Cheviot drainage development and meltwater channels, including glacial and fluvio-glacial phenomena and
deposits. (Based largely on the work of R. Common and C.M. Clapperton.)

confluent ice masses parted, (c) when meltwater from the ice-free higher ground flowed down beneath the stagnant ice around the hills, and (d) a period when a large lake was impounded on the north side of the hills by the Tweed ice, while on the southern side the present pattern had already been established. Esker and kame systems occur up to 275 m, but are absent south of the River Breamish. Many of the channels started as subglacial chutes, and then became englacial tubes, before being superimposed onto the ground below as the ice melted. The steeper channels, some of which are rock gorges 10-30 m deep, are interpreted as subglacial. In many instances the pattern of channels is complex, with bifurcating channels occurring.

In the first phase three sets of channels all converged on the Breamish valley. Sediments associated with meltwater deposition extend from Wooler southeast to the Breamish valley, forming eskers and kame complexes with kettle holes; bedded deposits are overlain by ablation or flow till in two places. These deposits merge into a terrace at the northern edge of the Hedgeley basin, forming in the second stage in Breamish glacial lake. Ice-contact slopes exist to the north, west and south, while to the east the terrace deposits merge into laminated silts and were originally a sandur deposit, building out into a glacial lake as the ice sheets parted and melted. The mid-Alun valley also once held a glacial lake, as indicated by laminated fine sediments and three deltas at 60 m. In the third phase drainage in the northeast part of the area changed from flowing southeast to flowing north to the Till valley, by which time the Hedgeley Lake had drained away. During the fourth stage glacial lakes formed around the sites of Wooler and Chatton at a level of 60 m, with stagnant ice in the Till valley over which meltwater drained eastwards. As the stagnant ice melted in the Till valley, the Milfield depression was flooded to form a large lake in which a large amount of laminated clay was deposited widely below 45 m. A proglacial outwash delta was built into the lake, sloping from 69 to 42 m at the mouth of the river Glen. The outflow cut the rock meanders of the Till valley northwest of Etal to the river Tweed, flowing subglacially beneath stagnant ice in the lower Tweed valley.

A further study of meltwater channel by Clapperton (1971)

deals with those of the eastern Cheviot Hills. He points out that meltwater channels are not common where ice moved parallel to the valleys. The commonest type is that superimposed from an englacial to a subglacial position. Complexes of eskers and kames occur in the low ground where ice became stagnant in basins and where thick till suggests heavily-charged basal ice. Both factors combined on the northern and eastern side of the hills, and much debris was carried up into the zone where meltwater streams could redistribute and deposit it as bedded sands and gravels.

Meltwater channels are of all dimensions up to features over 30 m deep, from those only 1 or 2 m wide and deep, and are cut in drift or bedrock or both. They usually occur in groups and often in valley heads and cols. Many cut across spurs as meltwater was directed parallel to the ice flow, but across the trend of the ground. A situation of this type occurs on the north side of the hills where Tweed ice was flowing east. The ice here deposited many drumlins and at their southern margin they are covered by fluvioglacial deposits, forming irregular belts of eskers and kames and sinuous ridges, or in places parallel ones. Kettle holes also occur. In the Teviot valley ice-contact deposits occur east of Hawick and are more continuous downstream of Kelso. Eskers and kames are extensive to the west of Etal on the River Till. South of Wooler and Chatton fluvioglacial deposits occur as far south as the river Breamish.

The drumlins of the Lower Tweed suggest heavily-laden basal ice. Some contain bedded material, and may indicate shaping of earlier fluvioglacial deposits by active ice. Most of the drumlins are of till, however, and borings suggest more than 60 m of till in places. These deposits provided material to be carried up into the ice and redistributed by meltwater to form the esker-kame complexes, which were formed englacially and later covered by ablation till as the ice stagnated away. This occurs south of Wooler. Ice contact deposits are not so extensive south and southeast of the Cheviots, where ice was derived from the Solway area. Firstly, this ice appears to have been cleaner and englacial moraine was lacking, and secondly, there are not suitable topographic localities to trap meltwater deposits, as water could flow freely with the grain of the country.

Northumberland In the Cheviot area the longitudinal profiles of the channels are mostly unidirectional in slope, although some are slightly undulating, with peaty hollows and low rock bars. In some south Northumbrian drainage channels, which have been studied in detail by Peel (1951) and later by Sissons (1958), the profiles are up and down. The East Dipton and Beldon Cleugh channels are situated on the northern flanks of the Alston block south of Hexham. The major point of interest concerning their origin is their humped longitudinal profiles, falling in opposite direction from a central col. Beldon Cleugh drains north to Devil's Water and south to Beldon Burn, while East Dipton channel, which is three miles long, drains west from a col at 127 m to Devil's Water and east for a greater distance to March Burn. At its maximum the East Dipton channel is over 61 m deep and Beldon Cleugh is about 50 m deep.

If the channels were cut by lake overflows the ice fronts require complex changes to allow the channels to drain alternately in either direction to cut the appropriate part of the longitudinal slope. Peel also puts forward the suggestion that the reverse-slopes are of secondary origin, cut by later streams, but their form does not support this view in his opinion, so that he tentatively supported the first suggestion.

Sissons postulated that the channels were cut by subglacial meltwaters. In order for this to take place ice must cover the area instead of a lake. Sissons showed that this was in fact likely, as the straight ice front previously suggested would not be probable on account of the great variation in thickness that would occur along its length as it passed from spur to valley. It is much more likely that ice lobes would press up into the valleys and they would provide the ice cover, beneath which subglacial meltwaters could flow uphill under hydrostatic pressure along parts of their courses. Thus the most likely explanation of the Beldon Cleugh is that it was formed by a subglacial stream, flowing uphill from the Devil's Water and then downslope to Beldon Burn.

Lancashire The Trough of Bowland [622531], a deep channel cutting across the main watershed of the Forest of Bowland is another impressive meltwater channel. It also slopes in two directions and the western side may have been cut by meltwater flowing uphill beneath the ice pressing against the hills from the west. This water could then escape and flow down the eastern ice-free slopes to cut the steeper eastern section of the channel.

Glacial meltwaters have also caused drainage channels on the edge of the Lancashire plain. The Whalley Gap which links the Calder to the Ribble through the Pendle-Mellor Ridge was probably used by meltwater from Lake Accrington, which formed during deglaciation. The ice must have reached at least 180 m in height above sea level. Water was turned north through the Whalley gap by glacial deposits in the Blackburn area, although the gap was also used by south-flowing water from Lake Accrington at an earlier phase. The river Calder has now become incised into the glacial outwash sediments in the gap, (Gresswell 1953).

Lakes were also held up in the Manchester embayment during deglaciation (Rodgers 1962). Evidence for their presence is seen in distinctive spreads of glacial sands and gravels, for example at Littleborough [940162]. These deposits have since been dissected. Dissection of the glacial deposits in the Mersey and Irwell valleys has also given rise to terraces, cut through flood gravels.

Durham In east Durham the Upper till ice, advancing from the north, held up a lake to the west against the higher ground of Magnesian limestone. Deposits of sand, 6 to 9 m thick and clays up to 18 m thick were deposited in this lake, which has been called Edder Acres Lake. The lake overflowed westwards through a channel cut 30 m through the solid rock, the intake of the channel being at 140 m. This channel may connect a little further south, with the large Ferry Hill Gap meltwater channel, which also cuts through the Magnesian limestone in a gorge 45 m deep. The Ferry Hill channel buried rock floor slopes down southwards through the main part of the gorge. There are many buried channels beneath the drift of County Durham, but it is not known whether these are earlier meltwater channels or modified preglacial valleys. It is likely that both types of valley exist. The buried valley of the Wear directed northwards towards the Tyne is one of the deepest cut. This old valley has steep sides and appears to have a graded course in the upper part at least.

At Escomb, one mile east of Bishop Auckland the rock floor of the buried Wear valley is at 55 m O.D. and the present river is at 73 m O.D. The subdrift valley floor falls to 40 m at Bishop Auckland, to between 0 and -4.3 m O.D. at Shincliffe, and to -21.3 m at Cocken Bridge, where the present river is at 12 m. It is at -43 m at the confluence with Chester Burn at Chester-le-Street and -57 m in the Team Valley Trading Estate. The course cannot be easily followed and the profile may be hump-backed below Chester Burn. The channel is mainly formed by fluvial erosion although glacial overdeepening is possible locally. It is as a result of glacial diversion that the present Wear valley flows to the sea at Sunderland, owing to the blocking of its old valley by drift.

The Bride moraine in the Isle of Man is dissected by a large number of drainage channels, which radiate approximately dendritically from the main ridge of the moraine. The largest is the Lhen trench [395990], which originally carried material south-westwards, but which has now been artificially drained to carry water northwards. The channels include marginal channels, directed mainly east-west parallel to the ice front, direct channels running perpendicular to the ice front to the south, and subglacial channels, trending northwards towards the ice front.

In interpreting the many meltwater channels that exist in Northern England it is necessary to bear in mind that various alternative methods of formation are possible. Where there is good evidence for large glacial lakes, such as in the Eden valley where lake deposits abound, direct overflows are likely to occur, but elsewhere evidence for large glacial lakes may not be present, and a subglacial origin for drainage channels must be considered.

Askrigg block Drainage channels of different forms and dimensions are common throughout the area. Many of those in the Pennine Dales have been described by Raistrick. Marginal channels are well developed along the slopes of the Pennine fault scarp. These are in general directed northwards towards Lake Eden at its various levels, forming conspicuous features between Croglin and Rensick, between Melmerby and Milburn, and further south between Hilton and Appleby. There are good examples of these channels behind Dufton and Knock Pikes, helping to give these hills their isolated conical form. The streams cutting these channels also deposited deltas in the lakes into which they drained. It is probable that all these channels were cut in a fairly short period of time by very large discharges of heavily loaded meltwater. They mostly have steep sides and flat floors, testifying to their rapid erosion by large volumes of meltwater. This form is well exemplified by channels cut in Swaledale by drainage waters associated with the main Stainmore-Vale of York ice margin, northwest of Richmond. Many of the channels are now dry, but some, such as Scandal Beck carry diverted waters.

The large volume of stratified sediments laid down by melt-waters show that much of their load was deposited in the area. Some of this material, such as that forming the kame and esker complex of northwest Durham, was probably associated with the decay of stagnant ice *in situ*. This is most likely to have happened in those areas that were furthest from the ice source. In this area the deposits generally become coarser upwards, clays leading up into sands and these in turn passing up into gravels, with a capping of clay with stones. These deposits were probably laid down in standing water either beneath or close to the margin of stagnating ice. Ice stagnation seems to have dominated ice dispersal west of the Lake District.

The stages of retreat of the Scottish ice front can be traced by means of the associated meltwaters. Sediments give evidence of an ice-dammed lake in Uldale at 135 m. The pattern of drainage channels is related to faults in the Carboniferous limestone and Borrowdale Volcanic Series (Shipp 1964). Submarginal channels occur on the west slopes of Black Combe and Muncaster Fell, as well as sub-glacial chutes and col gullies. Deltaic deposits were laid down in tunnels and cavities beneath the ice rather than in lakes in this area, indicating ice stagnation (R.A. Smith 1967). Stagnant ice also appears to have been responsible for the de-glaciation features around Lake Ennerdale. These features include subglacial and englacial channels and deposits, while some marginal lake deltas also occur (Huddart 1967).

R. Clarke (1967) has described in detail the glacial drainage features of the Malham Tarn area. These include erosion of col channels and chutes, as well as deposition of kames south of the Tarn. The kames contain ice-wedge pseudomorphs, indicating periglacial conditions, probably during Zones I and/or III.

5   Periglacial and postglacial features

Periglacial

During the waning phases of the glacial period, when much of the
land surface was not covered by ice, the climate must have been
severe and periglacial features are likely to have been formed.
L. Tufnell (1969) has discussed the range of periglacial phenomena to be seen in Northern England. He describes frost-
shattered bedrock in limestone and sandstone in the Alston
block, while there is also evidence of frost shattering below till in
the Cheviots. Blockfields occur on Cross Fell, Little Dun Fell and
Knock Fell in the Alston block, and these are probably entirely
due to periglacial processes. Nivation benches occur in north
Yorkshire and congelifluction deposits of head, consisting of
angular debris are found in the Howgill Fells, Lake District and
Pennines. In places terraces are formed of these deposits, one
type forming garlands, and a second terraces, as at Middle
Tongue Gill in the northern Pennines. Block streams and screes
are common. The screes are still moving, and stones have been recorded to move up to 30 cm/year in the Lake District by T.N.
Caine (1963b). Ploughing blocks that push up the soil in front of
them and have been found at 450 m in the Lake District and
820 m on Dun Fell.

Stone polygons, including fossil tundra polygons occur on
Moor House Reserve, Cross Fell, High Scald Fell, and are up to
15 m across on Knock Fell, although they are only of the order
of a metre across on Little Dun Fell. Sorted polygons occur
mainly in the Lake District. The fossil ones probably date from
the Devensian period. There are some small modern stone stripes
and larger fossil ones. The former are 7 to 10 cm on Great Dun
Fell. At present they form above 600 m and are more common in

the Lake District, where the material is more suited to their formation. Caine has located 45 examples of stone flats, in which
the larger stones occur on the surface above smaller ones, which
in turn overlie fine material above bedrock. These are currently
developing. Thufurs have been observed by Tufnell (1966) on
Great Dun Fell at 5 m. They are hummocks 20 cm high, and
they probably require a climate more severe than the present to
form. Although a considerable variety of forms have been observed forming currently, these are all small features compared
with the larger fossil ones, formed under harsher conditions.

The Moor House National Nature Reserve in the northern
Pennines is one of the coldest areas in England, and L. Tufnell
(1971) has studied the association between present day snow
patches and morphology in this area. Snow banks lie on sub-
summit benches and hollows on Great Dun Fell. They can be
60 cm thick and are transverse, longitudinal or circular. They are
related to wind patterns, which replenish the snow at suitable
sites by blowing. The features on which the snow collects include
altiplanation terraces and nivation hollows. Processes are associated with freeze-thaw activity, and needle ice formation was
observed, assisted by dampness due to recent snow melt. Frost
cracks were also observed. Composite block movement was also
taking place, with differential velocities of blocks and soil; sometimes the block moved faster and sometimes the reverse. Small
mass movement terraces also occur especially just below long
lasting snow patches. Linear cracks form parallel to and up slope
of semicircular hollows, forming back walls, for example on the
southwest slopes of Great Dun Fell. A piece 117 x 46 x 38 cm
had slipped down the back wall. Melt water erosion in wet soggy
ground below the snow patch was also observed. Snow is a major
element in current erosion processes, and the normal snow cover
period at the higher elevation is about 100 days each year.

The landforms associated with ploughing blocks have been
described by L. Tufnell (1972), from observations made in the
northern Pennines. The block ploughs through the soil making a
mound downslope of the block and a hollow upslope. The blocks
move under present frost action in the Moor House Nature
Reserve; the largest block with recorded movement was 2.5 m by

1.4 m, extending 70 cm above the ground. Of the 500 blocks observed 90% were between 30 and 120 cm long, and 17% had their long axes perpendicular to the slope. Only 6.2% of the depressions exceeded 30 cm depth. A variety of mound types was identified. Recorded movement was slow, at 5 to 7.5 cm/year, and was variable from year to year. Frost is the main cause of movement, which takes place mainly between mid-August and early April, in winter. The ploughing blocks occur mainly on grassy slopes, where the regolith is thick enough on slopes between 10 and 30 degrees, although lower gradients of 4 to 5 degrees sometimes have ploughing blocks.

Present-day nivation processes in the Cheviot area have been discussed by R. Clark (1972). Sites that today accumulate snow include a site east of Hedgehope at 720 m and southeast of the Cheviot at 815 m, both being areas previously shaped by nivation. The Bizzle and Hen Hole show nivation processes even better, and in 1963 drifting snow remained for 260 days at these places. The sites are at or above 680 m, or 70 m above the upper edge of the Bizzle and 260 m above the lowest nivation hollows of the late glacial cold climate era. Other phenomena in years as cold as 1963 include solifluction on frozen till. When thawing had occurred to a depth of 25-35 cm, thawed soil over a stretch of 40 m slid over the frozen ground below onto the valley floor. Alluvium was also eroded from the river banks as the ice floes broke up and snow drifts against the banks caused them to collapse, thus eroding silt.

The periglacial features vary in age with locality. Thus in the Isle of Man where ice only covered the higher hills in the Older Drift times periglacial features may date back to the Main (Devensian) glacial period of the mainland. Similarly most of the Cheviot hills were not covered by ice during the later phases of glaciation in Zones I and III, when the Lake District carried quite considerable ice cover. The higher parts of the Lake District are likely to be those in which modern periglacial features would be found. These different areas can be considered in turn, so that the more recent features will be described last.

The subdued forms of most of the high ground in the Isle of Man suggests that periglacial solifluction has been active during the long period since the whole area was over-run by ice. The character of the till exposed in the Druidale stream [354879] suggests that most of it has moved down the slopes into the valley bottom. An indurated till layer, lying parallel to the valley side, indicated that the upper layer had moved by solifluction into the valley bottom as the stream cut down into the drift.

The remains of possible pingos in the Isle of Man have been described by E. Watson (1971). They consist of depressions without ramparts and are of the open system type. They are associated with the glens that drain northwards towards the western side of the lowland area of the northern Isle of Man, including Glens Mooar, Wylling, Dhoo, Sulby and Auldyn. These glens end in gravelly fans, and on the fan surfaces are elongated depressions with ponds, well exemplified on the Ballaugh fan. The largest pond in 130 m by 90 m. Their orientation varies from 120 to 140 degrees north. They have been interpreted as dead ice features. The fan material is locally derived. The ice buried beneath the fan material could have been discrete lumps of pingo ice, as the fan surface is otherwise plane. The absence of a rampart could be due to ploughing as they occur on agricultural land, and are now ploughed to the edge of the pools. The evidence of pollen suggests that the pingos formed in Zone I or earlier in tundra conditions of permafrost. The orientation perpendicular to the slope suggests an open system pingo origin. Other indications of periglacial activity are faint traces of altiplanation terraces on the northern slopes of South Barrule [257759] and Snaefell [397880], while the V-shaped valley of Ravensdale [360915] has a considerable fill of angular head on the valley slopes, into which small gullies have subsequently been cut. One problem of the glaciation of the Isle of Man is the extent of ice incursion into the mountain area. One view, advanced by Lamplugh, suggested that clean ice sheared over the upland, to account for the lack of erratics in the upland area. The major part of the upland area, however, is covered both on interfluves and in the valleys by drift. Solifluction terraces are common in the valleys, and they result in valley side asymmetry. Fabric studies by G.S.P. Thomas (1971) indicate that the deposits are the result of periglacial solifluction activity. All the preferred orientations lie parallel to the valley slope. The period of deposition is probably Devensian, although the possibility remains open that the deposits represent a reworking of an earlier and more extensive spread of glacial deposits, dating from an earlier glaciation that could have overrun the whole island, but the evidence is not conclusive.

In Glen Dhoo, on the west side of the valley, and facing east, there is a good example of a periglacial dell [345903]. This had the form of a shallow hollow in the hill side and was made conspicuous by its bracken covering, surrounded by heather. It probably formed by nivation processes operating around a snow patch in the hollow. The head of the Glen Dhoo valley does not appear to have been glaciated but the lower part of the valley is the most U-shaped in the island except for the major transfluent trough. It is therefore, possible that an ice tongue pushed up the valley southwards from its mouth forming an intrusive glacial trough. Solifluction lobes were apparent on the northern slopes of Slieau Freoaghane [340884] a little further south.

Nivation hollows have also been reported by Common on the higher parts of the Cheviot hills, and he considers that the Henhole and Bizzle are probably features due mainly to nivation processes although Clapperton considers them to be corries. Another area in which similar features occur is in the upper Eden valley (see fig. 5.1) and on the higher south-facing flanks of Wensleydale. The Eden valley features have been described as corries by Rowell and Turner (1953), but they are more likely to be the result of periglacial and nivation processes. There is evidence in this vicinity that solifluction was active in the cold period of Zone III, and these features probably date from this time. Walker has described a section in Lunds (see p. 98) where Allerød, Zone II, organic deposits are overlain by solifluction material, only a mile or two from the corrie-like features. Thus it seems likely that periglacial processes were operating in this area while small glaciers developed in the Lake District.

The features are best developed on the slopes of Mallerstang and their back walls are formed of Millstone Grit, while the shale beneath has facilitated the development of the features. Many

angular blocks of grit lie at the base of the steep grit wall. A lobe
of material has moved down the hillside, spreading outwards
from ridges leading up to the outer edge of the back-wall cliffs.
The form of the lobe resembles solifluction features. Their stones
show no preferred orientation, which is commonly found in

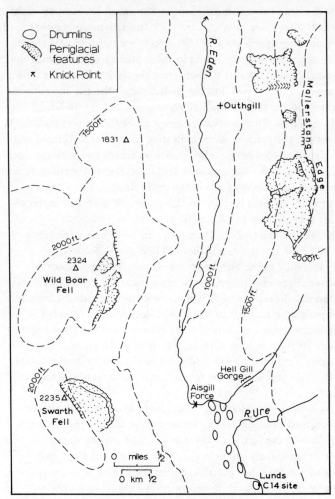

Fig. 5.1 Distribution of late-glacial periglacial forms in Lunds, upper
Eden valley. Carbon 14 site at Lunds is indicated.

moraines. The upper ridges are probably protalus ramparts, and were formed of material accumulating on the flanks of semi-permanent snow banks. The roundness of the sandstone stones from the protalus rampart was measured, using Cailleux's round-ness index, and compared with that of the same type of stones from a drumlin at Outhgill nearby. The values for samples of 50 stones were respectively 86 and 175, the difference between them being significant at 99.9% level (t = 8.0 for 98 df). These values suggest that the stones in the protalus had not undergone glacial erosion because of their great angularity. When the snow melted, water seeped into the shale beneath the grit and softened it, promoting the tendency to solifluction and landslides.

Similar solifluction features, now grassed over, are found in many of the Pennine dales, indicating that in the lateglacial and early postglacial periods the climate was more severe. Sometimes the solifluction is accompanied by landsliding and small elongated lakelets occasionally form in the landslide scar. There are examples of these lakelets on Mallerstang. The organic material that accumulated in them indicates that the earliest deposits in the lake belong to Zone IV, which confirms that the features could have formed during the cold late glacial Zone III.

It is only in the highest areas that periglacial processes are active at present. However, the summits of the higher Lake District hills reach a sufficient altitude for some small examples of periglacial features to form now. Hollingworth (1934) has drawn attention to some of these features, and has shown that some of them at least must have formed in the postglacial period as they are found on mine debris. The mines were worked about 300 years ago, so that the features must have formed since that date.

On the top of Helvellyn examples of small and not very well developed stone circles can frequently be seen on the flat stony surface. These features consist of a ring of coarser stones surrounding finer stones in the centre. Where the slopes are slightly steeper the circles become stone stripes. It seems likely that these features can be reformed in a single season owing to their small dimensions. The stripes are about 30 cm apart and the circles only about 1 m in diameter. Their presence does indicate, however, that frost activity is capable of moving stones at about 900 m elevation when the material consists of a suitable mixture of stone sizes.

Other features, described by Hollingworth, which are the result of periglacial processes operating at present, are the turf-banked terraces that occur on some of the northern Lake District hills. These again are the result of thawing and freezing during the winter period. These features consist of an almost bare tread, with a turf-covered rise to the next flat and they seem to be becoming more widespread as grazing by sheep and other causes tend to reduce the effectiveness of the vegetation cover.

Caine (1963) has recorded contemporary frost heave in the Lake District at a height of 750 m on Grassmoor. The differential heave between coarse and fine stripes was found to be up to 40 mm, with a mean value of 30 mm, after a cold spell in which there was a freezing period of 3 or 4 days. It was found that this was the minimum that would produce heave in the site studied. Ice formed in thin layers parallel to one another.

Postglacial
The period that can be called the postglacial in Northern England only covers the last 10,000 years, but this period is sufficiently long for certain minor modifications to have taken place in the landscape. When the ice retreated the slopes in some areas were not in adjustment with subaerial conditions. Adjustment has sub-sequently taken place largely by scree formation. This process would have been most active soon after the ice retreated from any area, because frost action in close proximity to the glaciers would have been active and this is usually an important process in scree formation. Glacial retreat also may help this effect by causing pressure release. This would provide the cracks into which the water could penetrate and freeze, thus disrupting the rock. Scree formation has been most active in the oversteepened valleys of the Lake District, the most heavily glaciated part of the region. The screes on the edge of Wastwater are particularly good examples. Profiles of these screes show them to be almost recti-linear as the lake at the base of the screes hides their lower slopes. In the Howgill Fells screes on the over-steepened slope of Yarl-

side [685975] have a concave profile. The steep slope is due to watershed breaching by ice below the corrie of Cautley Crags. The concavity is the result of non-removal of material from the base of the scree. This scree is now stabilised at least in the lower part. Other stabilised screes are found beneath the steeper lime-stone scars in the Dales.

Another process that has operated at intervals in the post-glacial period is the formation of peat on the damper uplands. Peat is widespread on the moors of the Pennines and the flatter summits of the Lake District, although the higher hills are too exposed for much peat to accumulate. It often buries tree stumps indicating that it was only in the wetter and cooler postglacial phases that conditions were suitable for its formation. Two different views concerning the causes of the current erosion of the peat have been put forward. M.M. Bower (1960, 1961 and 1962) has suggested that the main cause for peat erosion is climatic. The erosion was found to be most intense and advanced in the higher, wetter parts of the Pennines where the peat is thicker.

J. Radley (1962), however, holds the view that the present erosion of the peat was induced by human interference with the vegetation resulting from stocking and burning. Peat is lost in the flatter interfluve areas by deflation and stream erosion, while stream recession in the steeper downslope zone is the main pro-cess. The modification, resulting from human interference, of the hydrology could lead to increased runoff and hence increased stream recession. The observations of V.M. Conway and A. Millar (1960) support Radley's view. They found that in small catch-ments of 4 to 8 ha at 520-610 m in the Upper Tees area variation in load of peat and silt varied from zero to 2.25 m^3/yr according to the state of drainage and burning operations.

While peat has been accumulating on the uplands, vegetation and sediment has been filling in the lakes on the valley bottoms. Most of the lakes held up by moraines in the Pennine valleys were shallow and these have all been filled in, with one exception, and now form flat flood plains, still liable to flooding. The exception is Semerwater in Wensleydale, but even this lake is now much smaller than it used to be. At its maximum it was

about 6.5 km long when it was probably ice-dammed and overflowed at a height of 390 m south of Addlebrough. It is now
barely 1 km long. The Lake District lakes and some of those in
the northern Pennines were originally much deeper than those of
the Askrigg block. They were true rock basin lakes and although
they show considerable filling, and often contain fine deltas and
alluvial fans, some of them, such as Wastwater and Windermere,
still are below sea-level in their deepest parts.

Blea Water is 63 m deep, which is deeper than most of the
corrie lakes. A detailed study of the chemical content of the
postglacial sediments in a number of the Lake District lakes by
Mackereth (1966) gives information concerning changes in the
environment. The postglacial sediments are normally 4 to 6 m
thick and they show comparable changes from lake to lake. The
sediments reflect the nature of the soil in the basins draining into
the lake. The change, particularly of carbon content, is associated
with variations in rates of erosion, an increase of carbon being
related to decreased erosion. The changes of erosion rates are
probably related to climatic change, and the relation between
rate of erosion and halogen and boron content, suggests that
greater oceanicity is related to increased erosion. The junction
between glacial and postglacial sediments has been dated at about
10,000 yr BP in Windermere. The carbon content increases
rapidly at first to a maximum and then decreases slowly. The
minimum erosion occurred from about 5000 to 9000 BP, with
steadily increasing erosion occurring from 5000 BP to the
present, during which period the carbon content decreased. The
rate of deposition also increased in the upper part of the Esth-
waite lake sediment, which agrees with increasing erosion. There
are thus three phases, one of decreasing oceanicity, then a minimum, followed by one of increasing rainfall, leading to greater
leaching, soil impoverishment and resulting increased erosion.

Many of the valleys show postglacial terrace formation, probably related to changes in load and discharge rather than to
changes in base-level. Most of the features so far mentioned are
the result of postglacial deposition, there are also some features
that are due to erosion. The most spectacular of these are the
gorges formed below the waterfalls. Falls such as Hardrow Scar

must clearly date from the retreat of the ice when they were initiated and the gorge that has formed as the falls have retreated indicates the amount of postglacial erosion. The gorge below Hardrow Scar fall is now nearly 1 km long. It is not possible to establish exactly when the ice retreated from this position, although it was certainly considerably more than 10,000 years ago. Nevertheless the waterfall has worked upstream fairly rapidly owing to the structure of the strata in which soft shale underlies hard, horizontally lying sandstone and limestone.

Postglacial events have caused considerable modification to the low ground of the Lancashire Plain. The till surface slopes down westwards at an angle steeper than that of the present surface. The valley of the Yarrow, flowing west from Chorley [580170], is filled with postglacial deposits. An important stage in the postglacial development in the Lancashire plain was the incursion of the Hillhouse sea. The transgression culminated in about 4950 BP. The sea was low when the ice retreated and then rose to this level in the postglacial transgression. It has left evidence of its presence in the abandoned cliff line at about 7.6 m O.D. The feature is well shown at Hesketh Bank where it is in the form of an old cliff in glacial till sloping up from 4.9 m at its foot to 9.1 m at its top. The old cliff line is well preserved between Mere Brow [420188] and Holmeswood [432167], at Shirdley Hill [362127] and at Hillhouse itself [342062]. At the latter point the cliff is cut in Keuper sandstone, although quarrying has destroyed the original cliff. The cliff line can also be seen in the Wirral, where it runs from north of Grange Hill [210870] to Moreton [260900] Bidston Hill [287900] and Wallasey [290930]. It is possible that the Wallasey area was an island at this time.

There is also evidence of the sea incursion in the Fylde, where the area north of the Wyre, known as Over Wyre, was flooded by the Hillhouse sea, the coastline of which can be recognised and is indicated on figure 2.8. The coast ran west to east south of Cleveleys [310440] and Thornton [343421] and then north to Preesal [370475]. Shingle was deposited at Preesal, marking the high water level. The sea also invaded the Ribble estuary and cut a cliff at Clifton [465303] and Newton [446306]. Lake Myers-

clough [500390] was a feature possibly associated with poor
drainage resulting from this high sea level. It is, however, possible
that this lake is an older feature, dating from the time of deglaciation, as a moraine-dammed lake. Rapid draining would have
occurred as soon as the narrow till barrier between it and the
Hillhouse sea at Skitham Gap [425435] or Trashy Hill [447744]
had been breached. Part of the old lake bed is now peat covered.

Much of the area seaward of the Hillhouse coastline is now
covered by superficial deposits associated with the sea and laid
down during its gradual withdrawal. The oldest of these deposits
is the Shirdley Hill sand. This is a high silica sand and can be
differentiated from the recent blown sand by the absence of
black particles, which characterise the recent blown sand. The
sand is incoherent, and yellow or white in colour. It abuts against
the till on the western side of the Hillhouse coastline. The sand is
in the form of beach sand in situ in places, but elsewhere it has
been redistributed by the wind to form dunes, as at Altcar
[320065], Barton [355090], and at Hillhouse. Blown sand also
extends inland of the actual coastline of the Hillhouse sea,
reaching an elevation of up to 120 m.

As the sea withdrew the offshore gradient must have become
very gentle as silt overlies the Shirdley Hill sand. This Downholland silt was deposited when the sea had withdrawn about 1.5
to 3 km and had become muddy. The silt overlies the sand near
the limit of the sand. The silt was deposited in the intertidal zone
and it contains *Scrobicularia*. At Formy Moss [319080] 17 m of
silt lies on 3 m of Shirdley Hill sand, although this thickness is
exceptional. A more usual thickness is 9 to 11 m.

Trees grew on the silt as sea level fell but drainage deterioration allowed peat to form, and in places this has been covered by
more recent blown sand near the present coast. The impedence
of drainage was probably partly due to the accumulation of
blown sand along the coast. Thus much of the Hillhouse beach is
now covered with peat, which buries the remains of the trees. The
peat is often between 2 and 3 m thick, and more in some places.
In some areas it hides the Hillhouse coastline. The peat forms the
Mosslands, for example Halsall Moss [340120]. The Moss is
below the high water level at present, and drainage is necessary

to make the land productive. Elsewhere alluvium forms the surface, as in the Alt valley.

These recent superficial deposits have affected the drainage pattern of the Lancashire Plain. The recent blown sand has no surface drainage, while the peat mosslands are artificially drained. The natural drainage has also been greatly disturbed by the glacial and fluvioglacial deposits. Shallow lakes occur in the blown sand where the water table rises above the floors of depressions amongst the dunes, as at Ainsdale-on-Sea [301130] and elsewhere amongst the Formby Hills.

The river Douglas, which rises in the Rossendale upland flows south, following a glacial meltwater channel to Wigan. At Poolstock [574045] it turns northwest through the high ground, ignoring lower ground to the south. This part of its course also follows a meltwater channel as far as Parbold [495108], near where it entered the Hillhouse sea at Rufford [460150] or south of Tarlscough [420130]. As Martins Bay silted up, when the sea retreated west, the Douglas seems to have been diverted north along its present course to the Ribble estuary. The Yarrow, which flows west from Chorley to join the Douglas north of Rufford, also follows a meltwater channel in its southward directed course to the east of Chorley. Its former lower course is indicated by a strip of gravel trending west. The gravel underlies peat in several places.

The Ribble valley has undergone changes associated with the sea level fluctuations of the postglacial period. Sea level was at first very low and as it rose to the Hillhouse level erosion took place inland, forming rejuvenation features in the Ribble flood plain and its tributaries. The associated knick-points are in till. Aggradation took place in the Ribble valley as sea level fell after the Hillhouse transgression. The aggradation was due to the very low gradient of the lower part of the river that was exposed as sea level fell. The offshore gradient (from 25 to -145 feet) was only 1:1300, compared with the present gradient between the 25 and 100 feet contours of 1:600. Erosion started again as the sea started to recover its level in rising to its present height. These changes in erosion and aggradation in the Ribble valley have resulted in terraces that reached a maximum height of 3.7 m at

Preston. These changes are not those normally associated with changes of base level owing to the abnormally low gradient of the lower Ribble estuary.

The postglacial development of lowland Lonsdale has been described by F. Oldfield (1960b). He examined the southern and eastern part of the Kent Estuary. His results are based on detailed pollen analysis associated with stratigraphical observations. Good pollen sequences are available in the saltmarsh deposits and peat bogs that lie between the limestone cliffs and the sea. These deposits all postdate the last ice advance. The evidence is largely derived from three sites, Hawes Water, Arnside-Silverdale Moss and Thrang Moss. The Hawes Water basin still contains a small lake around which lacustrine deposits occur. These deposits form a platform of dried-out calcareous marl deposited under freshwater conditions when the lake was larger and the water level higher. A belt of fen occurs to the south and west. A rock barrier separates the Hawes Water Moss from Silverdale-Arnside Moss, the latter two being separated by a much lower rock bar. These mosses contain postglacial, clay-silt deposits that contain *Cardium edule* shells, thus indicating a marine transgression into these mosses. The marine material is overlain by freshwater swamp, fan and finally raised bog, which has since been reclaimed or cut for peat.

The deposits at Thrang Moss are rather similar to those of Hawes Water. Dates were obtained from some of the organic material. The oldest deposit is a coarse gravel followed by a clay, both contain no organic remains and were probably deposited under glacial conditions. The overlying silty clay contains some organic remains suggesting a birch tundra vegetation. A deterioration of the climate is then indicated by a decrease of organic remains. This was possibly a period of treeless tundra, belonging to zone Ic, correlatable with the Aberdeen Readvance, the date being about 12,000 yr BP at the end of this phase. The next deposits show a climatic amelioration, with birch becoming reestablished. This milder spell is probably the Allerød period of Zone II. Further marginal solifluction marks the deterioration of Zone III and the proportion of tree pollen declines. This cooler period dates from 10,750 to 10,250 yr BP. The floral evidence from Hawes Water suggests that this area was probably relatively favoured during the Zone III cooler spell. The succeeding deposit marks the beginning of the postglacial period in Zone IV. However, the environment that has changed most rapidly during post-glacial time is the coast.

F.A. Hibbert et al (1971) have studied the vegetation succession at Red Moss near Horwhich, Lancashire [SJ 631101]. Carbon 14 dates through the Moss range from 4370 B.P. at a depth of 114-116 cm to 9508 B.P. at 325-330 cm. The vegetation assemblages are as follows:

Quercus-Alnus starts	5010 ± 80 yr B.P.
Quercus-Alnus-Ulmus	7107 ± 120 yr B.P.
Pinus-Corylus-Ulmus	8196 ± 150 yr B.P.
Corylus-Pinus	8880 ± 170 yr B.P.
Betula-Pinus-Corylus	9798 ± 200 yr B.P.
Betula-Pinus-Juniperus	9508 ± 200 yr B.P.

6   The coast

In some areas the coastal forms are entirely recent, but in others
there is evidence of older coastal features. The whole area has
been affected by the changes of sea-level that have taken place
during and since the glacial period. The earliest evidence of a
higher sea-level is found in the Easington raised beach of Durham
[444453] which occurs at a height of 27 m. Its included shells
have been dated at more than 38,000 years old it occurs between
the Upper and Lower till of Durham and is thus interstadial or
interglacial in date. Common (1954) supports the views of
Woolacott and Anderson that sea-level has been up to 60 and
46 m in late and postglacial time. This would imply that the
Northumbrian and possibly also the Durham coast has undergone
considerable isostatic recovery.

There is good evidence round the coast for a sea-level at least
7.5 m higher than the present during the postglacial period,
following a lower sea level when forests, now submerged, grew
below the present high water level. Specific examples of the evidence for changes in sea-level during the lateglacial and postglacial periods can best be mentioned when the particular coast is
described. Northern England has three distinct coastal units that
can best be discussed separately. These are the North Sea coast,
the Irish Sea coast and the Isle of Man coast.

The North Sea coast of Northumberland and Durham
It is on this coast that the evidence for a high lateglacial sea-level
has been found. Field work supports Anderson's view of a water
surface at +58 m. It could, however, possibly have been a lake
dammed up in the coastal embayments by Scandinavian ice in
the North Sea. The overflow would have been over a col between

the Tees and the Swale, its level falling as the outlet was lowered to 43 m. Smith and Francis (1967) cite evidence for a higher sea-level in south Durham in lateglacial times at a height of +25 m O.D. A planation surface near Hartlepool [492351] cuts across the Upper till and Middle sands and was probably formed after Zone I. Its sedimentary cover includes marine shells. Sea-level then fell below its present height to at least – 15 O.D. and peat, now associated with submerged forest, formed. Antlers in this peat have been dated at 8100 to 8700 ± 180 years BP. The 25 m coastline must be older than this; if it were marine it suggests that isostatic depression could have been 91 to 107 m, which would require an ice thickness of 274 to 320 m, which is a reasonable amount. Since the period of the submerged forests sea-level has been rising on the whole.

The coast of Northumberland and Durham runs in a fairly straight north-north-west to south-south-east direction with only relatively minor indentations. These become rather more marked north of Newcastle, where the rocks reaching the coast are more varied. The Durham solid rock cliffs are nearly vertical and con-sist of Magnesian limestone, varying between 15 and 45 m in height. They are however capped by thick drift in the south and are incised by steep postglacial valleys known as 'denes', such as Hawthorn Dene and Castle Eden Dene. These deep narrow valleys are cut mainly through drift, but some cut down into the Magnesian limestone.

North of the Tyne the cliffs are generally low and the head-lands occur where harder rocks run out to sea. Coal Measures outcrop between Newcastle and Amble, and Millstone Grit between Amble and the mouth of the Aln. Not all the coastline is formed of solid rock, however, and many of the broad open bays are filled with drift, the solid rock being at a considerable dis-tance below sea level. The Tyne is cut down to – 43 m in a rock trench, Sleekburn to – 28 m and there are two valleys below Druridge Bay cut to depths greater than 15 m, one lying east-west, the other north-south, and the Tweed at Berwick has a buried rock gorge descending to – 43 m.

The study by Anson and Sharp (1960) of the rock-head sur-face from borehole data has revealed three broad east to west valleys. One, entering the centre of Druridge Bay with its base more than 42 m below O.D., is an earlier mouth of the Coquet as suggested by Woolacott. It is a deep precipitous valley. The second channel is related to the Lyne to the south, and the third still further south is another major feature, near the modern Sleetburn more than 15 m below sea-level. It lies a little to the south of the line of the Wansbeck and probably carried both this river and the preglacial Blythe. The three remaining channels are directed north-south and are probably filled up meltwater channels. Whitburn and Whitley Bays are old valleys blocked by drift.

The coast between the Tyne and Alnmouth consists of low rocky headlands where the harder strata of the Coal Measures and Millstone Grit outcrop and broad sandy bays, usually backed by dune-covered drift. Between Berwick and Alnmouth the solid rocks of the coast consist of the Lower Carboniferous strata and the dolerite Whin sill adds variety to the coastal scenery. It forms the low cliffs north of Bamburgh and higher columnar cliffs, on which the castle of Bamburgh is sited. The sill also outcrops in the low, rocky Farne Islands a few miles offshore. The headlands at both sides of Embleton Bay and that at the southern end of Beadnell Bay are formed of Whin sill, while the northern headland of the latter bay is a basalt dyke. The small harbour of Craster is eroded along a fault. Between Budle Bay and the Tweed solid rocks outcrop only for a few miles south of the Tweed. These belong to the Scremerston Series and dip fairly steeply. A well developed wave-cut platform has been eroded in front of the low, till-capped cliffs in places. Till forms the basis of the coast between Cheswick Rocks [040475] and Budle Bay and nearly all of Holy Island is drift covered.

Accumulation forms are best developed in this part of the coast. Holy Island consists of three islands linked with shingle ridges and a dune-covered northern projection. A recurved spit has grown near Castle Point. Ross links to the south are formed of till and only reach 3.7 m above sea-level, although the seaward side is raised by dune growth to more than 18 m. Windblown sand has accumulated in dunes, usually of low elevation along a considerable length of this coastline. Dunes are extensively formed particularly along the drift sections such as from Cheswick Rocks south to include Ross Links, Budle Point to Seahouses, and in the broad bays of Beadnell, Embleton and Druridge to the south. The widespread distribution of sand dunes on a coast with a prevailing offshore wind testifies to the abundance of sand, probably the result of extensive sandy drift deposits offshore and to the recent changes of sea-level.

Accretion on the coast has taken several forms. Along much of the coast there is a beach. In the south in Durham the beach is narrow and fairly steep and is broken by headlands so that material cannot travel readily alongshore. However towards the south the beach has been artificially raised and widened by the tipping of coal debris in the sea, as at Horden [450420]. The dis-

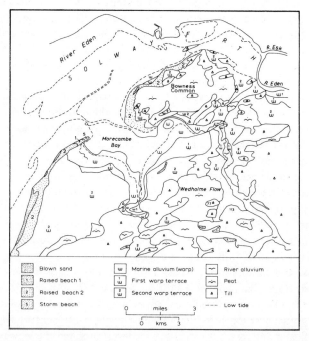

Fig. 6.1 *Above a*) Coastal features, including raised warp terraces of the southern side of the Solway Estuary. Based on the Institute of Geological Sciences. *Opposite b*) Former courses of the Irt and Mite Rivers in west Cumbria and other coastal features.

tribution of this material shows clearly the generally southerly movement of material on this coast. Marsden Bay north of Sunderland is a good example of an isolated small beach which is composed of fairly coarse sand that responds to changes in wind and wave conditions as illustrated in the profiles in fig. 6.1c (King 1953). North of the Tyne the beaches are narrow and short until Druridge Bay is reached. The beach here consists of very coarse sand, but it has a ridge and runnel profile, thus suggesting abundant sand supply. The movement of beach material is to the south on this stretch of coast as shown by the slight diversion south of the stream mouths. Nearly all the wide bays have broad sandy beaches, although there is a shingle storm beach in Embleton Bay and at the southern end of Beadnell Bay.

The most extensive zone of coastal accretion has grown up in the shelter of Holy Island. In Budle Bay and Lowmoor Point [095400] opposite Holy Island shelter is sufficient for sand and

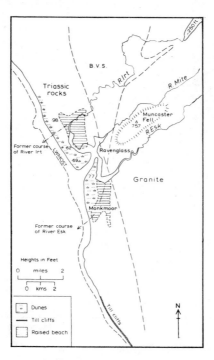

silt to accumulate around salt marsh plants, which include *Puccinellia, Salicornia, Suaeda Maritima, Aster tripolium* and some clumps of *Spartina townsendii*. These marsh areas are sheltered by Holy Island and the offshore barriers and spits associated with it. There are a series of offshore barriers between

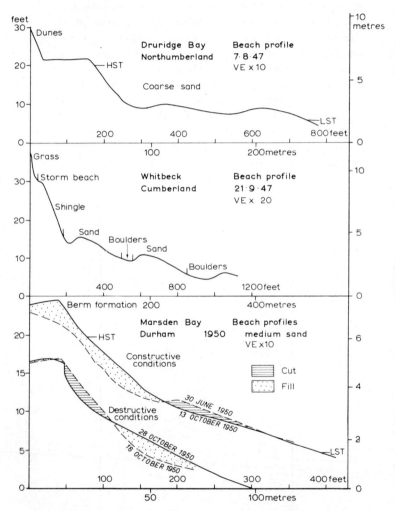

Fig. 6.1 c) Representative beach profiles (see fig. 1.1 for positions).

Cheswick [065458] and the western end of Holy Island. Ross Links has grown outwards at both of its seaward extremities to form a hammer-headed spit. The form and orientation of these features reflect the pattern of the long, refracted swell that has built them and which comes from the north. Swell coming in from the northeast between Holy Island and the Farne Islands would be least refracted in the centre of Ross Links and, therefore, highest here and longshore currents might develop towards the zones of greater refraction on either side. This would help to account for the growth of the spits in two opposite directions. The southeasterly spit shelters Budle Bay and allows the growth of salt marsh within it.

J.A. Galliers (1970) has given an outline account of the coastal geomorphology of Holy Island. The island appears to be comparatively stable in outline, as indicated by the close correspondence between the outline of the earliest map of the island of 1610 and the present map. The Snook Neck extends the island 1.2 km westwards from its northwest corner. Most of the island lies below 15 m, although the highest point on a dolerite dyke outcrop is double this, and the dunes reach up to 21 m. The Snook and Snook Neck are recently formed and consist of dunes overlying a low gravel ridge, and the dunes continue across the whole of the northern part of the island. The southern part of the island is covered mainly by till, although other drift deposits also occur, rarely exceeding 10 m in thickness, and overlying truncated Carboniferous rocks. The east coast is characterised by a narrow, but fairly continuous zone of beach gravels, while the northern coast is sandy, with rocky headlands between bays. There are also gravel ridges in the southeast of the island at Castle Point; these gravels and those of the Snook area are relatively stable. The Castle Point feature is a low gravel terrace of sub-rounded to rounded gravels, about 3.6 m above sea-level, although on the seaward side a ridge rises to 5.5 m above sea-level. This ridge consists of unweathered gravels, whereas those of the terrace are weathered; the outer ridge still undergoes occasional movement. There is a rock platform along the eastern shore, overlain by gravel and boulders and backed by low cliffs of drift and sedimentary Carboniferous rocks. The Snook area also rises to about 3.6 m in gravel ridges, but here they are overlain by dunes, in ridges rising to 10 m and crescent-shaped mounds 10 to 12 m high. There are also irregular forms. The highest point in the dunes reaches 23.8 m above sea level, with most of the dune crests exceeding 15 m. The long dunes are aligned almost east-west, but others at Snipe Point run southwest to northeast, and at Coves Haven they trend northwest to southeast. Sand for the dunes is derived both from the sand ridge to the north and north-west, and the Holy Island sands to the south. Most of the dunes are symmetrical in shape.

The Irish Sea coast of Cumberland

The tidal range is very much greater on the Irish Sea coast than on the North Sea coast of Northern England. On the former it varies between about 7.3 and 7.6 m at spring tide, while on the latter the spring range is from 4.3 to 4.6 m. Thus the beaches exposed at low water are considerably wider on the Cumberland coast than on the Northumberland coast in the same type of beach material.

Solid rock outcrops only at rare intervals on the foreshore north of Workington, there being one or two outcrops just north of Maryport. These rocks belong to the Coal Measure Series, which underlies the coast as far south as Whitehaven. South of this point the Triassic St Bees sandstone outcrops at intervals along the coast but along most of it the solid rocks are hidden beneath drift. The only significant outcrop along this stretch of coast is that in the vicinity of St Bees Head. Apart from a few short stretches to the north, only in this part of the coast is beach material lacking on the foreshore.

In the Solway the combined estuaries of the rivers Esk and Eden consist of a channel between 1.5 and 3.0 km wide at high tide, but at low tide wide sand banks emerge. Considerable areas of sandy salt marsh, consisting of 90% sand, on which good turf grows occur in the Solway.

There is evidence on the Solway shore of changes in sea level in the form of raised shingle beaches and raised salt marsh deposits. Peat bogs lying on the raised marsh terraces form the 'flows' such as Wedholme Flow [220530] which are character-

istic of this part of the coast. The marsh deposits consist of
laminated sandy loam, mainly turf covered. There are two raised
terraces of warp, the higher and more extensive can be traced
beneath the raised beach shingle at one place. This relationship
points to their contemporaneity. A good exposure of the raised
beach is seen at Grune Point [143568] extending to Beck Foot
[090493]. This beach and the second warp terrace are at about
9.6 m. The character of this area suggests uplift continuing until
recently. This phase of high sea-level must have been preceded by
one of lower sea-level in which forests grew below present sea-
level and were submerged by a rise in level. The warp terraces
mark slight halts in the fall of sea-level from the maximum transgression. The higher raised marsh rises from 7 m in the west to
8.2 m in the east and the lower lies between 5.5 and 6.4 m (fig.
6.1a).

The maximum of the postglacial transgression occurred about
650 to 1000 years earlier in the north, where isostatic recovery
initiated earlier regression and greater subsequent uplift. D.
Walker (1956) suggests that the sea-level started to recede
between 7000 and 6650 BP in the Solway area, where the subsequent fall has been about 5 m. He also (Walker 1966) has made
a detailed study of the pollen stratigraphy of Bowness Common,
Glasson Moss and Glasson shore on the Solway coast of Cumberland. Sea level in this area rose from –4 m in Zone III to lay
down deposits at +7.2 m O.D. in early Zone VIIa, and at +8.8 m
later in this zone. Sea level did not reach – 3 m before the end of
Zone III. On this part of the Cumberland coast the maximum
transgression occurred about 7000 BP, and it lasted until about
6600 BP. Greater isostatic recovery in this northern area appears
to have accelerated the start of the regression by as much as 650
years. Sea-level has fallen by about 4.5 m in the Bowness area
since Zone VIIa. At the other end of this stretch of coast in
Morecambe Bay the culmination of the transgression occurred at
about 6000 BP and sea-level has since fallen about 2.7 m. At
Ravenglass, 68 km south of Bowness in the Solway, the fall is
given as 3.3 m by Walker. A little further north at Drigg [046985]
peat outcrops on the foreshore and lies beneath raised beach
shingle at the back of the beach. The peat belongs to the Zone

VI-VIIa transition. Two samples of peat from the foreshore at
Drigg have been radiocarbon dated. The lower sample, collected
between 0.41 and 0.73 m O.D. was dated at 6720 ± 120 yr BP
(Y 2600). The upper sample, which consisted of wood taken
from the higher level peat deposit at 6.60 m O.D. was dated
6200 ± 140 yr BP (Y 2602). The higher level peat immediately
underlies a raised beach shingle deposit at 6.60 to 7.33 m O.D.
M.C. Pearson examined the peat sample for pollen and established a Zone VIIa flora. The peat accumulated over a period of
at least 500 years, according to the radiocarbon dates, and during
this time extended over a considerable vertical range, as sea-level
was rising to the maximum transgression. As the shingle probably
represents a high spring tide deposit, sea-level must have reached
about 3.7 m above its present height at Drigg [046985]. These
results agree with Walker's work. At Silecroft [120812] further
south, a raised storm beach crest was 4.6 m above the present
spring tide level and 4.1 above the highest tide level. This indicates a past sea-level about 4.3 m higher. Still further south at
Hodbarrow [182781] near Millom, shells were collected in a
raised beach at 8.7 m above O.D. This implies a fall of sea-level of
about 4.3 m. These levels are rather higher than those given by
Walker, and the difference may be due partly to the type of
coastal feature studied and its relation to mean sea-level.

The main area of accretion on this coast is in Morecambe Bay
[165565], which has gained 404 ha between 1864 and 1946.
This bay was formed by a post-Roman breach in the shingle
ridges. Marsh accretion does not occur throughout the area and in
places erosion scarps 0.3 to 0.6 m high separate the marsh from
the foreshore. The modern marsh lies at about 4.6 to 4.9 m and
is dominated by *Puccinellia* and *Salicornia*, the latter being the
first coloniser. On balance, along the Cumbrian coast erosion is
probably exceeding accretion at present, partly as a result of the
effect of man-made structures.

The movement of material into the Solway by wave action
along the coast would help to account for the great extent of
sand banks in the present estuary and also the great width of the
raised terraces of warp in this vicinity. The present beach is very
wide between Silloth [105535] and Dubmill Point [076458],

being 2 km wide for part of this distance. The beach consists mainly of sand, although shingle often occurs at the top of the beach and outcrops of rock and patches of boulders also are found. Wave action is not very effective because of the great width of the beach. Beach material is also probably derived from the erosion of the drumlins that reach the coast in this area.

The width of the beach decreases steadily to less than 800 m in Allonby Bay, where the coast becomes more open and wave action can be more effective. The beach is still mainly sandy, but similar banks of shingle and rock outcrops occur. Part of this stretch of coast is backed by the raised beach, but this, like the modern beach, is much narrower here. The beach narrows steadily southwards as far as St Bees Head, where it vanishes altogether. The raised beach is not so conspicuous south of Workington where it lies at 4.3 m above the modern beach.

South of the high cliffs and narrow rock platform of St Bees Head the beach again widens and consists of sand and shingle, backed by drift cliffs nearly all the way to Hodbarrow Point near Millom. The direction of coastal drift changes at St Bees Head being northwards to the north of the headland and southwards to the south. The river Ehen has been diverted southwards for nearly two miles (3 km) by the growth of a narrow shingle spit. The Irt also turns south behind a wider sandy spit, but the Esk turns north to join the Irt and Mite in a joint outlet. It appears that formerly the Irt had a separate mouth. These deflections, on cartographic evidence, appear to have taken place in the last 300 years. The Esk also probably flowed south formerly through Monk Moors [085924]. Dunes form an important element of these spits. The orientation of this stretch of coast suggests that there is not much longshore transport of material in the vicinity of the Esk estuary. The beach becomes gradually sandier southwards and the boulders on the foreshore become fewer before the Duddon estuary is reached, (see fig. 6.1b and c).

The Irish Sea coast of Lancashire
F. Oldfield (1960) has considered the evidence for a postglacial transgression along the coastal fringe of lowland Lonsdale. The presence of marine clay in the Mosses of Silverdale and Arnside

confirms an incursion of the sea. Levelled values give heights of
5.75 m and 5.79 m on marine clay surfaces. Another indication
of the high sea-level is the presence of notches at the foot of the
limestone cliffs around the bays. These notches are found at
heights between 4.9 m and 5.38 m O.D., most values falling close
to 5.0 m. Most of the notches are now protected from further
marine erosion by saltmarsh stretching in front of the old cliff.
The cliffs have suffered some subsequent degradation by subaerial processes.

The results of the levelling suggest that the height of the
highest high tide would be a minimum of 5.8 m on the open
coast and 6.7 m in the more restricted waters of the Kent
estuary. The date of the transgression has been fixed by pollen
analysis at Zone VIIa. By pollen Zone VIIb the level had fallen a
little to 2.1 m above its present height. The highest level must
have been between 5.8 and 9.15 m O.D. Radiocarbon dating
places the transgression between 5750 and 5950 yr BP or
possibly a little earlier. This is earlier than suggested by previous
workers by 400 to 900 years. An earlier date, compared with the
dates for areas further south, could be due to the effects of isostatic recovery in the Lonsdale area.

The same area in Morecambe Bay has also been studied by
R.K. Gresswell (1958), whose observations also extend over a
wider stretch of the Bay. The northern part of Morecambe Bay
consists of several deep estuaries of the rivers draining from the
southern Lake District. There are three bays in the otherwise
smooth coast line between St Bees and the Mersey estuary. These
are the Duddon Estuary, Morecambe Bay and the Ribble Estuary.
Morecambe Bay is 16 km wide and 27 km deep, half of its area
drying out at low water. There is no structural link between its
northern and southern sides. On the south side of the Lake
District are the estuaries of the Duddon, Greenodd and Kent.
They all contain flat ground around their heads at about 6 m
O.D. These flat areas are raised shorelines. Their inner margins
are of four types, (a) precipitous slopes in solid rock, (b) steep
slopes exceeding 1:5 with a veneer of moraine, (c) degraded
slopes of less than 1:5, and (d) obscure boundaries due to movement of surface material. The last type is rare. The pure clay is at

least 6 m deep in many places, consisting of blue-grey silty clay, becoming grey-brown below 1.25 m. Sandy silt also occurs and sand increases at depth towards the open sea. Most of the elevations on the top of the clay were within the range 4.4 to 4.7 m O.D., the mean height being 4.65 m. Out of 126 values 110 fell between 4.4 and 5.2 m. The elevations were the same in all the estuaries.

Seismic surveys showed that in the Lyth valley of the Kent the bedrock lay at a minimum depth of 61 m below the clay surface on Lord's Plain [470870]. The estuaries show evidence of heavy glaciation; roches moutonnées and drumlins occur in the Greenodd estuary. Peats occur in sections through the deposits and pollen of all zones from I to VIIa has been identified in Witherslack Hill between Winster and Lyth.

Gresswell confirms that the transgression occurred in Zones VI to VIIa, the Boreal-Atlantic transition period. The raised beach at 4.6 m is a little lower than the Hillhouse beach at 5.2 m in southwest Lancashire. In the latter area waves would be higher and the tidal range greater. The estuaries must have been awash by about 1 m at high tide, so the high water level would have been about 5.5 m O.D. This agrees with the height of the wave-cut bench at 5.8 m on Winder Moor. The isostatic rise of 0.3 to 0.6 m, more in north Lancashire compared with the south of the county, could be accounted for partly by greater isostatic recovery in the north.

When the ice melted the Isle of Man was linked to the mainland, but this link was severed as the sea rose to the maximum postglacial transgression. At one stage peat grew to a level of −8.33 m O.D. at Bootle [322962] ; allowing for the tidal range, this figure means that sea level must have been 12.2 m lower. During the last 3000 to 4000 years sea level has risen at a rate of 0.3-0.4 m/century. The present high water is +5.2 m O.D. The modern coast has been influenced by the slow rise of sea-level following a withdrawal after the postglacial maximum transgression, which formed the Hillhouse coastline and its northern extension into the bays on the southern side of the Lake District.

A detailed study of the land/sea-level changes in northwest England has been made by M.J. Tooley (1974). Severe flooding occurred in 1720, 1833, 1907 and 1927. In southwest Lancashire 41 km^2 is below high spring tide level and requires artificial or natural protection. The coastlands below +6 m O.D. consist of perimarine, lagoonal, tidal flat and sand dune areas. Peat in Morecambe Bay occurs at – 11.13 to – 16.40 m O.D. Carbon 14 dates indicate that between 8925 ±200 and 7995 ±80 yr B.P. sea-level rose from – 20 to – 15 m O.D., causing transgression in the Bay and the estuaries of the Kent and Leven. The present coast was crossed at Heysham. The Irish Sea must have been closed earlier than Mitchell thought. In southwest Fylde peat occurs at – 11 to – 9 m O.D. in two valleys cut in till. Peat with charcoal at −11.13 m O.D. is of Flandrian I c/d date, about 8200 B.P. with approaching marine conditions. Clays and silts are intercalated with peats and sealed by 3 m of blown sand with a peat layer in it. The date suggest ten marine transgressions in southwest Fylde, at Lytham giving the following sequence:

Lytham	I	9270-8575 B.P.
	II	8400-7800
	III	7600-7200
	IV	6885-6025
	V	5950-5775
	VI	5570-4800
	VII	3770-3150
	VIII	3090-2270
	IX	1560-1380
	X	about 830 B.P.

Downholland Moss in southwest Lancashire between the Ribble and Mersey shows a complex pattern of marine transgression in the Flandrian II and early III periods. The first reached 7 km from the present coast to – 0.27 m O.D. The sea-level curve derived from these data oscillates up and down. It reflects global eustatic changes and regional subsidence of sedimentary basins, as well as local factors due to biogenic sediment consolidation and tidal range variations. Rapid rises are followed by still-stands or falls. The pattern consists of 12 steps, (1) between 9200 and 8500 sea-level rose from – 20 to – 9 m O.D. at 1.5 cm/year, and then fell nearly 1 m when Lytham I occurred. (2) from 8400 to 7800 B.P. sea-level rose in Lytham II. (3) from 7800-7600 a rapid rise from −9 to −2 m O.D. at 3.5 cm/year took place. (4) Lytham III was a period of slow rise and then a fall from 7600 to 7200. (5) In Lytham IV a rise of sea-level caused a transgression. (6) sea-level rose to +2 m O.D. with the marine limit at 5775 B.P. (7) a low point of 0 m O.D. was reached at 5470 B.P., then a rise followed to +3 m O.D. with a further fall from 5000 to 4800 in Lytham VI. (8) a low level of +2 m O.D. and a rise to +3 m O.D. occurred at 4500. (9) Lytham VII occurred at this time. (10) a low sea-level of +3.5 m O.D. in Lytham VIII, followed by a rise and fall to +4 m O.D. at 2270 B.P. (11) the marine limit in Lytham IX was at 5.4 m O.D. nearly 1600 B.P., and by 1370 B.P. the level was +4.6 m O.D. (12) fossil dune slacks suggest a maximum of +5.5 m O.D. about 805-830 B.P. Since 800 B.P. sea-level has fallen from +5.5 m to +3.8 m O.D., the equivalent of mean high spring tide at St Annes-on-Sea. The evidence tends to support the fluctuating curve of the Flandrian transgression of Mörner and Fairbridge, sea-level having risen three or four times above the present sea level in the last 4000 years. The very rapid rise of sea-level in Lytham III is related to the disintegration of the Laurentide ice sheet, when Hudson Bay became free of ice. Nine distinct marine transgressions have been identified with a tenth in the Dark Ages. This very detailed study agrees well with data obtained from the west coast of Cumberland a little further north. (Andrews, King and Stuiver 1973).

The coast between the Duddon Estuary and Wirral in the south consists of a series of deep embayments, already mentioned, and stretches of smooth coast. In the south estuaries are also important, those of the Mersey and Dee being major features of the coast. The deep embayments around Morecambe Bay owe their existence to the scouring and over deepening action of the Lake District glaciers, which eroded their valleys below sea level, as the ice flowed down from the Lake District hills into the Irish Sea. The southern estuaries also owe their depth to ice erosion, but in this instance the ice formed intrusive troughs, as it concentrated to force a way through the narrow gap between the Welsh and Pennine highlands.

Between the estuaries the greater part of the coastline of the Fylde and southern Lancashire is formed of drift and postglacial deposits, forming a good example of a low coast. On this soft coast marine erosion has been dominant, at least in parts, as sea-level has risen. The cliffs at Blackpool were about 3 miles further seaward, but they have been pushed eastwards as the sea has risen. Erosion, before sea defence works were undertaken, was at a rate of about 2 m/yr. Coastal protection works in the form of sea walls have prevented recent erosion at Blackpool. At times the walls have been built seaward of the backshore to widen the promenade. Sea walls at Blackpool were built between 1895 and 1899, but between 1910 and 1911 they were set back, indicating true erosion to be at a rate of 3 m/yr. Twelve miles of this coast-line are now protected by sea walls. Sea walls have been extended northwards to Bispham [308402] because the sea walls further south, built to protect Blackpool, prevented material reaching Bispham along the shore in this area, where the beach drift is to the north. The Bispham beach, therefore, started to suffer erosion. The northerly drift is also seen in the spit at Rossal Point [311477] near Fleetwood. The spit prolongs this stretch of coast northwards across the river Wyre. Salt marsh is growing in its shelter in the Wyre estuary.

The coast between the Wyre and the Mersey is sandy. The estuaries of the Wyre and Ribble, however, accumulate finer sedi-ment, giving rise to areas of salt marsh, as in the estuaries further north around Morecambe Bay. The Ribble marshes have been partially reclaimed around Hesketh Bank in three stages, in about 1830, 1850 and 1880. Dredging is necessary to keep the estuary open. The rapid filling of the Ribble estuary is due to both natural and human causes. The form of the estuary and the large tidal range are important, and also the rapid spread of *Spartina townsendii* over the marsh area. On the human side reclamation and channel control have helped to account for the infilling. The tide floods into the Ribble estuary for 4½ hours and ebbs for 7½ hours. The flood streams flows at 2.4 m/sec and the ebb at only 1.60 m/sec. Material carried in can be deposited and is not washed out again by the ebb. The range at spring tide at Preston is 8.2 m and 7.9 m at Lytham St Annes, showing an increase in range up the estuary. The estuary is sheltered, a fact that also helps to account for infilling. There are 1730 ha of unreclaimed marsh in the estuary, and on this *Puccinellia maritima* is a common plant. Most of the natural marshland is on the south side of the main channel, which has been regulated and artificially straightened. The artificial channel, which is dredged, lies near the north side of the estuary. *Spartina* was planted on the south side in 1936 and has since spread. *Puccinellia* is used for grazing on the marshes. The marsh develops through the following sequence: Cryptogamic zone (not extensive in this area, and consists of algae, lying below the high water of the lowest tide) → *Salicornia* with or without *Spartina* → *Spartina* → *Puccinellia* with *Spartina* → *Puccinellia* → *Festuca* → *Juncus*. Further reclamation could be carried out on the marshes in this estuary.

Between the Ribble estuary and the Mersey is a stretch of sandy coast along which Formby Point is the most outstanding feature. This point has undergone erosion at the rate of 4.6 m/yr between 1906 and 1925. This is due to the direction of longshore drift being away from the point in both directions. The material goes to add to the accretion in the Ribble estuary to the north and the Mersey to the south. Accretion also takes place at Southport, north of Formby Point. Accretion took place at Formby Point in the nineteenth century at the rate of 3.7 m/yr between 1845 and 1892. The cause for the change may have been a cutting off of sand supply from offshore, due to dredging of the Mersey Bar. Sand was supplied to Formby along a 4 km stretch of the offshore area. Erosion also occurs at Blundellsands [300999] due to the lowering of the backshore as a result of changes in the course of the River Alt across the foreshore.

This stretch of coast has been studied in detail by R.K. Gresswell (1953) who has analysed the processes operating along it. The large amount of sand present on the coast has given rise to dune formation in places. Dunes occur south of Southport where they are advancing slowly, although trampling causes some blowouts. It is in this area that recent experiments have been carried out in dune stabilisation by spraying the dunes with a solution that prevents blowing, while marram grass, planted before the spraying, has a chance to take root and form a protection over the bare sand. Between Ainsdale [299129] and Woodvale [310110] the dunes are 4 km wide. At Woodvale the rate of

accretion is between 1.55 and 3.35 m/yr. Erosion starts 800 m
north of Victoria Road, Freshfield [290085] and reached a rate
of between 4.0 and 10 m/yr for the period from 1934 to 1938.
Accretion begins again south of Formby Point. The southerly
movement south of Formby Point has led to the diversion of the
outlet of the river Alt 6.4 km to the south to flow across the
beach into Formby Channel. Its outlet has varied over a distance
of 4.8 km between 1689 and 1950. Erosion has occurred at
Blundellsands since the turn of the century, at 10 m/yr from
1913 to 1920 and at 11.6 m/yr between 1920 and 1928.

One characteristic of the Lancashire coast between Barrow in
Furness and the Dee estuary is the exceptionally large tidal range,
which exceeds 6 m at mean tide and approaches 9 m at spring
tide. This large tidal range accounts for the wide extent of the
foreshore at low water, and the extensive sand banks and shoals
that dry out at low water in the estuaries. The beaches are also
exceptionally wide, exceeding 1000 m along much of the coast.
The average gradient of the foreshore, therefore, is gentle, with a
slope of 1:165 for the foreshore and 1:80 for the backshore.
There has been a slight increase in this gradient between 1892
and 1925, due to coastal erosion and reclamation. The sand on
the coast comes mainly from the glacial deposits, and was derived
from the Triassic and Carboniferous rocks mainly. The present
rivers, particularly the Mersey, which is closely controlled, probably bring down relatively little sand at present.

The south Lancashire coast is only affected by waves generated within the Irish Sea. The largest fetch is to the west and is
200 km, there is 150 km to the northwest, 130 km to the west-
north-west and 55 km from the west. The coast is mainly orien-
tated perpendicular to the maximum fetch, and where this has
not yet been achieved erosion and deposition are causing the
coast to tend towards this orientation. Forty % of the stronger
winds come from west-north-west, and 35% from the west. The
dominant waves come from a direction of 277 degrees. This
direction can be related to the direction of the beach ridges,
which are a characteristic of the foreshore on this coast. The
beach ridges north of Formby trend at 24 degrees and the coast
at 32 degrees. South of Formby the ridge trend is 167 degrees,

where the coastal trend is 157 degrees. At Formby Point ridges and coast both trend at 182 degrees. These trends account for the erosion at Formby, as material drifts away from the Point to both directions owing to the oblique wave approach of 17 degrees to north and 20 degrees to the south of the Point. The direction of approach of the dominant breakers is from 277 degrees in deep water and 272 degrees in shallow water. The erosion at Formby is sufficient to supply the material that accretes at Ainsdale and district. Little accretion is now taking place at Altcar [280050].

Gresswell is of the opinion that some material must be supplied to this coast via the offshore banks from the Dee estuary and North Wales. Different parts of the coast have been accreting or eroding at various periods, probably as a result of minor fluctuations in mean wind directions. Variations in off-shore features have also probably played a part. The rate of supply of sand from below low water has decreased or even ceased since about 1906, resulting in erosion since this date at Formby Point. This change could be related to dredging at the Bar, and the concentration of the Mersey tidal current in the Crosby Channel by the building of training walls. The walls may have increased the ebb tide and so prevented sand crossing the channel to reach Formby. The position of the Alt is responsible for erosion at Blundellsands in that it has lowered the beach level and prevented longshore drift, even though it has been directed artificially straight to the sea. Accretion occurred at Formby until this century, a process that must have been due to more sand reaching the coast from offshore than was drifted away from the Point along the foreshore.

The presence of ridges and runnels on the wide sandy shores of Lancashire south of the Lune is due to a surfeit of sand on these beaches, a legacy of the postglacial rise of sea-level following the regression after the maximum postglacial high sea-level of the Boreal-Atlantic period. Glacial and fluvioglacial processes have provided this wealth of sediment in the sand grade. The large tidal range associated with the low gradient due to the abundance of material provides the very wide foreshore. The lack of long swells in the sheltered Irish Sea, in which the modal wave period is only 5 seconds, also helps to account for the ridges. Where the waves are short the equilibrium beach gradient will be relatively steep, so that the waves will tend to build ridges on the foreshore with a swash slope gradient steeper than the flat overall gradient. The process of ridge building takes place most effectively at the levels at which the waves operate for longest period in the tidal cycle. These are at the mean tide heights. This relationship between the position of the ridges and the tide heights can be demonstrated on the beach near Blackpool where the waves approach at an angle of only 4 degrees to the shore.

On this beach, observations carried out between 1943 and 1945 showed that by far the most consistent ridges remained more or less fixed about the positions of mean high neap tide, mean low neap tide and mean low spring tide. The mean low neap tide ridge was the highest because the parabolic form of the overall beach gradient made the greatest difference at this point between the equilibrium gradient of the swash slope and the overall beach gradient. Where the ridges lie almost parallel to the shore, as at Blackpool and Formby Point, they remain more or less fixed in position on the beach; where however, they lie at an angle to the shore, as north and south of Formby Point, they tend to move inland on any one profile as the whole ridge is moved bodily in the direction of longshore drift of beach material.

The deep estuaries form a contrast to the open ridge and runnel beach along the Lancashire coast. The Mersey is of particular interest from the point of view of its shape and the processes operating within it, and also because of its importance for shipping both to Liverpool and Manchester, via the Ship Canal. Solid rock outcrops to form the narrows between Liverpool and Birkenhead on the Wirral, the resistance of the rocks being responsible for the shape of the Wirral peninsula. The lowest level of the channel is 68.5 m southeast of Runcorn in the Weaver valley. The Mersey rock channel deepens southwards away from its mouth. The inner Mersey estuary has an area of nearly 78 km^2 and because of the large tidal range, a very large tidal prism flows in and out through the narrow outer estuary, which is less than 1200 m wide. This powerful tidal stream prevents silting in the outer estuary, thus maintaining a deep water channel to the port of Liverpool.

Dredging is necessary to maintain the Manchester Ship Canal because it requires navigation through the lower part of the upper estuary although most of it is by-passed. More than half the upper estuary dries out at low water and many sand and mud banks emerge. Silting must be prevented as far as possible in the upper estuary. Price and Kendrick (1963) discuss the problems of siltation in the upper Mersey estuary and describe tidal models built to solve these problems. The outer estuary consists of one deep channel 18.3 m deep at low spring tide, which has a range of 8.2 m, but there are three main channels in the upper estuary. Field observations made preparatory to model design showed that there was a net drift landward on the bed for a variety of tidal ranges, the volume moved increasing with the tidal range. The salinity difference between sea and river water increased the effectiveness of the flood tide at the expense of the ebb. The conclusions reached suggested that at the beginning of the century equilibrium had been reached, with material coming up the narrows into the upper estuary from the sea, but not in such quantity as to cause serious loss of capacity in the upper estuary. Since then training walls had been built beyond the Narrows and these were shown by model tests to reverse the net direction of sediment transport in the Narrows and in the bay beyond, where sediment now moved inland. This material found its way into the upper estuary, seriously reducing its capacity. Between 1906 and 1960 the loss of capacity was 79 million m^3, causing a reduction throughout of 0.85 m. The change was caused by training works which prevented the free movement of sediment up and down the flood and ebb channels in the bay, concentrating the flow into the ebb channel. The training works achieved their main aim of keeping the approaches to the port of Liverpool open, but they had deleterious effects in the upper estuary from the point of view of maintaining channels through it. Another aspect of the training walls in the Eastham Channel [365820] is that although they helped to maintain the approach to the Manchester Ship Canal at Eastham Lock they prevented the free meandering of Eastham Channel and this process helps to prevent siltation.

The form of the Mersey estuary, with its narrow entrance, contrasts with the relatively straight sided Dee estuary and the strongly tapering Ribble estuary. The Dee estuary has not been controlled artificially and rapid siltation has taken place. Most of the Dee estuary now dries out at low water and salt marsh growth has been very extensive within the estuary: indeed schemes to reclaim the whole estuary have been put forward. Dredging is also necessary to maintain navigation up the Ribble estuary to Preston.

The large estuary of the Leven and Kent and Lune, which together form Morecambe Bay is also tending to silt up, and large areas of sand emerge at low water. Recently studies have been carried out to examine the feasibility of building a barrage across the bay. Experiments carried out with sea-bed drifters by A.W. Phillips (1969) suggest that movement of material in the bay under the influence of tides, waves and wind drift is dominated by the net tidal drift. The direction of movement resulting from the net tidal drift was found to predominantly in a westerly direction in the area to the north and west of the Lune Deep, which lies near the southern margin of the bay. During periods of strong easterly winds, however, this direction of movement may be halted or reversed. Most of the drifters released in the entrance and middle of the bay moved towards the northwest shore. The most numerous recoveries were made on a spit at the southeast tip of Walney Island, lying close to the seaward end of the Walney channel. Walney Island is one of the areas where accretion is taking place most rapidly in Morecambe Bay, and the drifter experiments suggest that the source of material is the floor of the bay, and the transport is achieved mainly by tidal streams, assisted by the stronger waves that accompany the prevalent and dominant westerly winds.

A later experiment, when drifters were released on a flood tide rather than the ebb as in the first experiment, produced rather different results. The ebb tide moved the drifters first to the outer part of the bay from where they could reach Walney Island and the northwest part of the bay. Those released on the flood tide moved first further into the bay, and most of them did not escape from the bay subsequently. In the later experiments most of the drifters were recovered from the banks within the bay and from its eastern shore between Heysham and Carnforth. The general conclusion reached was that within the bay the movement is mainly north and northeast towards the head of the bay, while at its mouth movement is anti-clockwise towards the northwest corner of the bay.

A study of the charts of the bay over a period of 123 years made by Kestner (1970) suggested that there is a cyclic movement of the sand banks and channels within the Bay. The situation of the banks at present seems to resemble that at the beginning of the period studies, indicating that a complete cycle may have run its course in the bay. He studied the 11 Admiralty charts surveyed between 1845 and 1968 of the approaches to Heysham harbour through Heysham Lake, the northeastern continuation of the Lune Deep in the southern part of Morecambe Bay. In this part of the bay, three deep channels extend northeast from the Lune Deep, with intervening shoals. The channel and bank nearest to Heysham have migrated steadily southeastwards during the 120 years of detailed surveys. The migration, at a mean rate of about 30 m/yr, has amounted in the whole period to a movement of the channel of 4580 m and of the bank of 3300 m. At first the movement of the bank, Clark Wharf Spit, towards Heysham Lake caused the depth to increase as scour became more concentrated, but continued movement overwhelmed the Heysham Lake with sand and rapid shoaling took place, reducing depths to less than 5.5 m at low water. This caused serious deterioration in navigation conditions. The movement of the channel and bank has also caused narrowing of Heysham Lake. The bank has now reached the centre of Heysham Lake, but is decreasing in volume steadily at present, Kestner considers it likely that the movements of the channel and banks will now repeat, Heysham Lake will start deepening again fairly soon, as the Clark Wharf Spit disappears, and the state at the beginning of the cycle of change is restored. A new channel and bank should start to move southeastwards once more.

The coast of the Isle of Man
The coast of the Isle of Man can be divided into two unequal

parts. No solid rocks outcrop between Ramsey past the Point of Ayre to Gob ny Creggan Glássey [298890], but the whole of the southwestern part consists of mainly rocky coast, with only small sandy or shingle bays. The spring tidal range round the island varies from 6.4 m at Ramsey, 6.1 m at Douglas, 5.5 m at the Calf Sound, and reaches the lowest value of 4.9 m at Peel. Even though the range is fairly high the beaches are nowhere very wide. This is because near Ramsey, where the range is greatest, the upper part of the beach consists of shingle and sand is only exposed at low tide. Near the Point of Ayre the beach becomes very narrow as it consists of large shingle and hence has a very steep gradient. It becomes sandier again further southwest near Jurby Head [343981].

Raised beaches near the Point of Ayre form a spread of shingle and sand. The Ayres raised beach deposits have been described by C. Ward (1970). They occur at 3-4 m above high water, which is 6 m O.D. Douglas. The fossil fauna are recent in character and the beach extends from Phurt in the east to Saltfield in the west. The raised beach deposits rest on a platform at above modern high tide and are obscured by a shingle storm ridge. Three basins with deposits of silt are separated by 150 m of shingle, which is well-rounded and dips at $10°$ to the north. The shingle is storm beach material, deposited on the seaward margin of the basins, which were undergoing sedimentation. The last basin is terminated by a large shingle storm ridge, which is the first in the Point of Ayre series. Lough Cranstal is possibly a kettle hole, connected by a meltwater channel. The raised beaches form two groups, the northern one striking at $065°$ and the southern at $075°$. The former is not parallel to the present coast and the latter is not parallel to the raised beach cliff behind it to the south. In recent years erosion has taken place on the east side of the Point of Ayre. Ridges have been added by progradation, rather than being due to a fall of sea-level, although they are now above the level of normal marine action. The back of the beach is probably pre-Neolithic. Where sand is available parabolic dunes have formed, with tails facing east or west.

The drift cliff north of Ramsey, which reaches a maximum height of 76 m at Shellag Point, has already been described on

pp. 89. Northwards the height falls off rapidly to the Point of
Ayre. The wide triangular area lying seawards of the Bride
moraine consists of a series of well developed raised shingle
ridges, which have become covered by blown sand at their inner
edge, (see fig. 2.6). These old ridges reach a height of about 7.4
to 9 m above the modern sea-level near the light-house [464048].
The ridges run at a considerable angle to those on the modern
shore, which cuts abruptly across them. The actual tip of the
Point of Ayre is growing outwards at a fairly rapid rate at present
by the addition of new shingle ridges, but a little further west the
old ridges are being truncated. These old shingle ridges probably
represent the same period of higher sea-level as that noted on the
Cumberland coast.

At Blue Point [393026] further west the raised beach takes
another form. Here it is an old drift cliff grassed over with a raised
beach platform several hundred metres wide between it and the
modern dunes and beach. Further south the old cliff has been
removed by modern erosion which has produced good sections in
the drift cliffs. At Glen Mooar [302894] the drift section
includes large rafts of tough till amongst stratified sands, with
tough till at the base of the cliff. The drift cliff is about 30 m
high in this area and the deposits were probably laid down by a
stagnant ice sheet.

In the southern part of the coast there is also some evidence
for a higher water level. At Niarbyl beach [200775] there is a well
flattened rocky islet offshore at a height of about 7.6 to 8.8 m
above local datum. There is good evidence in Port Erin bay that a
marine-cut rock platform was formed earlier than the deposition
of the drift that fills most of the small bays around the south
coast. Another section is exposed in the Calf of Man sound
[173665] at the southern tip of the island. The rock here has
been planed off at about 7.5 m above modern high tide level.
This platform was covered by stratified deposits and overlain by
what appeared to be till and angular head material, the whole
forming a flattish platform 11.3 m above high water. Gresswell
has interpreted these deposits as delta sediments laid down in a
proglacial ice-dammed lake, formed when ice lay in the sea
around the island. However, it is doubtful if a rock platform

could be cut under these conditions. The platform may have been cut during a period of higher sea-level before the last ice advance in the area. Another younger, and lower, raised shingle beach was found in Port Mooar on the east coast near Maughold Head [488910] ; this feature was 3.7 m above modern high water or about 7.0 m above local datum. An old valley draining into the bay was filled with till on which the shingle rested, indicating its younger age, which probably correlated with the Point of Ayre features.

The modern cliffs have a similar form along much of the coast, a good example of the type being found in Bulgham Bay [457855] north of Laxey. The land at about 150 m is gently undulating, then there is a steep, straight slope down to the top of the short, vertical modern cliff. A similar form is seen around much of the south coast, except that the flattish surface above the cliff is at a lower height. On parts of the southwest coast, however, the uniform slope has a much greater vertical height, for example on the seaward side of Cronk ny Arrey Laa [224746] . In this instance it is over 30 m high in places, ending above the low vertical cliff formed by modern erosion. A little north at Niarbyl the slope above the modern cliff is much gentler, because in this area it is cut on drift, which overlies the rock outcropping at sea-level. A gravel platform at 12.2 to 13.7 m near Niarbyl has been interpreted as a delta in an ice-dammed lake by Gresswell. The drift forms a gentler modern cliff slope above the near vertical rock slopes.

Only the lower part of this type of cliff profile is directly affected by modern marine erosion, the bulk of the cliff being formed by subaerial processes. The cliffs were probably initiated during a period of lower sea-level, when the marine influence was absent over the part of the cliff now above sea level. The relatively sheltered situation of the Isle of Man in the Irish Sea may help to account for the limited amount of wave erosion on the cliffs. Marine erosion and cliffing are on the whole more effective on the exposed west coast, which would support this suggestion. The more rapid erosion currently taking place occurs in the drift cliffs north of Peel, particularly in the vicinity of Jurby Head. Beach material must move north along this coast and the supply from the rocky coast to the south is small. Sand eroded from the drift cliffs must move mainly offshore, while the shingle moves northeast to build up the shingle ridges of the Point Ayre. There is thus a considerable variety of coastal features along the shores of the Isle of Man.

7   Conclusion

Northern England lies within the Highland zone of Britain, and Palaeozoic rocks outcrop much more extensively than those of younger age. The area covers a wide range of landform types, which illustrate admirably the relationships between structure and rock type, on the one hand, and on the other, between these two elements and the landforms. The geomorphological map, fig. 7.1, attempts to show the distribution of some of the more distinctive elements of the structure and the landforms of the area. It contains several distinctive types of upland scenery and structure. The Lower Palaeozoic rocks of the Lake District include a considerable range of rocks and the structure is complex, while the Pennines provide very interesting contrasts from many points of view, with their very different structure and rock types. Yet both illustrate the dependence of morphology upon material. The upland areas are fringed by scarplands and separated by a variety of lowland zones, in which superficial drift deposits are widely distributed.

The Lake District and Pennines are separated by one of the most important major structural features of the British Isles, the great capital sigma shaped system of faults, which include the Stublick faults, the Pennine and Dent systems and the Craven faults. Along much of their length these fault systems separate the stable blocks of the Pennines from the subsiding basins around them. The presence of granite beneath the Pennines provides an explanation for these contrasts. It also shows how the deeper structure influences both the long-term sedimentation pattern, and hence the rock type, and the present day relief. The character of the uplifted and warped summit surfaces is thus intimately involved. The cyclothem type of sedimentation is very characteristic of the Pennines. It accounts for the alternating rock types of the central Pennines, very well exemplified in the Yoredale Series of Wensleydale and the other Yorkshire Dales. The Yoredale strata account for the distinctive landscape of scars and broad undulating plateaux type moorlands.

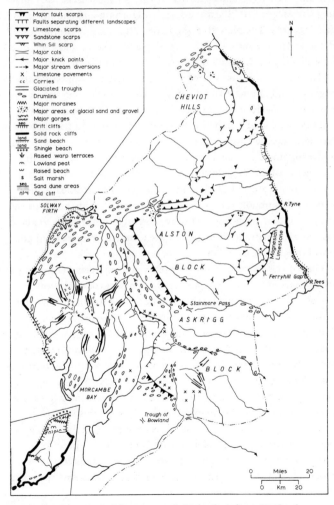

Fig. 7.1 Some aspects of the geomorphology of northern England.

Around the margins of the upland areas are the characteristic fringing scarps. Around the older rock cores they consist of Carboniferous rocks, such as those of the Lake District fringes and the Cheviot borders. There are also the Coal Measure scarplands of Durham and Northumberland. The harder rocks of the Mesozoic and New Red sandstone also form conspicuous scarps, including the Magnesian limestone scarp of Durham and the Eden Valley scarps. The New Red sandstone strata also underlie some of the lowland zones, such as the Solway lowlands and the Lancashire Plain, as well as the northern part of the Isle of Man.

The Carboniferous system outcrops extensively in Northern England, and amongst the distinctive rock types occurs the most massive and widespread strata of limestone in the country. The limestone areas of northwest England are renowned for their excellent karstic forms, which provide a different and fascinating landscape, including such well-known features as the limestone pavements of the Ingleborough area, the pothole of Gaping Gill and the dry waterfall of Malham Cove. The subterranean landscape of this important karst area adds another dimension to the scenery of Northern England. Cave research in northern England has revealed many interesting features and led to important geomorphological conclusions.

One of the most difficult problems in deciphering the geomorphological development of an area is to assess the effect of processes operating during the long period of Tertiary time. The erosion surfaces and river pattern provide some useful information. The conclusions to be deduced by a study of the drainage pattern and the denudation chronology can, however, rarely be considered definitive, and there are many problems of interpretation. There is, nevertheless, good evidence in Northern England for the existence of a summit surface that has recently been uplifted and warped. The quantitative analysis of this surface provides an example of the use of trend surface analysis technique in geomorphological study. This method is open to criticism, but in this instance the results can be related to the structure, and this in turn, to the deep-seated causes of the structure.

The Alston and Askrigg blocks of the central Pennines, where there is a strong structural control on landscape development, form a marked contrast to the Howgill Fells and the Lake District. These two adjoining highland zones consist of strongly contorted Lower Palaeozoic rocks, some of which are of relatively homogenous material from the erosional point of view. Thus any flatter surfaces in these areas must be the product of erosion, owing to the lack of structural control. The smooth rounded hills of the Howgill Fells and southern Lake District form a strong contrast to the scars and flat summits of the Yorkshire Dales.

The drainage development of Northern England illustrates well many fundamental concepts. The streams drain both to the west and the east coasts, and include excellent examples of radial and trellis drainage. The former pattern occurs in the Cheviots and the Lake District in a modified form, and the latter in the Northumberland coastal zone. The Howgill Fells provide interesting examples of drainage diversions related to the law of unequal slopes, first enunciated by G.K. Gilbert. The suggested history of drainage development of this area illustrates fundamental concepts of geomorphology, as well as providing many convincing examples of river capture on both large and small scales.

In nearly all aspects of the landscape of Northern England the details of the scenery are strongly influenced by the many and varied effects of the glacial period. The ice sheets and glaciers that repeatedly advanced and then retreated over Northern England have left their mark, although the effects of the earlier advances have been obliterated or blurred by the more recent ice advances. The last major ice advance to affect the whole area was the Devensian, so that many details of the landscape are directly the result of this glaciation.

Northern England provides some good evidence of the earlier ice advances. The very thick glacial sequence revealed in boreholes in the northern part of the Isle of Man provides valuable records of past ice advances, which still pose problems of interpolation. The cliffs of the northeastern part of the island reveal intriguing glacial structures associated with the Bride moraine. On the east coast of Northern England evidence in the form of Norwegian erratics is found to establish that the great Scandinavian ice sheet once reached as far as the British coast. Later, however, the local British ice was powerful enough to keep the Scandinavian ice offshore.

The paths followed by the glaciers can be traced in places by the occurrence of distinctive erratics in the glacial deposits. There are several very characteristic rocks outcropping in Northern England that provide useful erratics. The small area of Shap granite outcrop is a good example. Rocks from this distinctive source have been traced far and wide, onto both the west and east sides of the Pennines. They were carried by the Lake District ice as it spread out through every available col, including the Tyne gap to the northeast, the Stainmore col to the east, and the Lune Gorge near Tebay to the south.

The degree of ice activity in Northern England varied considerably according to local conditions of both snow and ice supply, and ease of glacier flow. There are many examples of very effective glacial erosion, which are particularly striking in the Lake District, especially where the Borrowdale Volcanic Series provide hard rocks of variable resistance to ice. The glacial landform include very good example of corries, U-shaped valleys with the rock steps and long, ribbon lakes so characteristic of the area. This area, lying near the west coast, have a high precipitation, which during the glacial period must have fallen largely as snow. The glaciers had open access to the low ground all around, and hence could flow freely and effectively, on account of their high accumulation rate.

The ice of the Howgill Fells and that over most of the Pennine area and the Cheviot Hills was less vigorous, partly owing to lower precipitation, and partly because it was hemmed in by more vigorous ice from the Lake District, Scotland and further afield. The local ice, nevertheless, was sufficiently massive to keep out the foreign ice. It was not moving fast enough, however, to effect much erosion except in locally favoured areas. Such areas include upper Wharfedale and Bishopdale in the Askrigg block. In the latter valley ice erosion has led to unusual drainage anomalies, whereby the main stream, the Ure, hangs about 50 m to its tributary, Bishopdale Beck.

Features of glacial deposition and fluvioglacial landforms also add variety and interest to many parts of Northern England. The thick drift of the northern part of the Isle of Man and the Lancashire Lowlands provide both a chronology of the Pleistocene and landforms of distinctive character, such as the Bride moraine of the Isle of Man. The drumlins of the Eden Valley and the Craven Lowlands diversify otherwise rather featureless area. They also give valuable evidence concerning the depositional processes that produce drumlins. Variations in their distribution, elongation ratios and their orientation all provide useful information of past ice flow patterns.

Meltwater features include impressive erosional forms, such as the deep channels of northern Northumberland, which have given rise to considerable discussion; they probably represent the operation of subglacial drainage systems. The depositional forms found on the northern and western margins of the Alston block, where eskers, kames and deltas were well represented, give evidence of different stages in the deglaciation of the area, where important drainage diversions resulted from glacial interference. The South Tyne was diverted to follow an easterly course to the North Sea, by glacial interference, during which Glacial Lake Eden grew to be an important ice-dammed lake. Its earlier westerly course to the Irish Sea was blocked by ice.

The last stages of glaciation in Britain are exemplified in the Lake District by the evidence of corrie glaciation dating from the post-Allerød cold period of Zone III. Corries were reoccupied and freshened by ice, the decay of which left the characteristic hummocky moraine in the higher parts of many of the Lakeland valleys. While the last small ice masses were creating or freshening the corries in the Lake District the rest of Northern England was suffering from a periglacial climate. The evidence for this is seen in a wide variety of periglacial forms, including major mass movement in the form of slumping. Nivation was active, creating protalus ramparts and other nivational features, such as nivation hollows. The former are exemplified in Edenside in the Pennines and the latter in the highlands of the Isle of Man, while in the northern lowland of the island fossil pingos have been reported. Even now in the higher parts of Northern England the climate is sufficiently harsh for periglacial processes to be operative on a minor scale. Stone circles and stripes can be seen on the higher

Lake District and Pennine hills, and frost heave has been recorded in recent years in these areas.

Postglacial modification of the landscape is actively progressing. It has led to the formation of impressive screes, for example around Wastwater in the Lake District, and the filling of glacial lake beds and coastal inlets in the Yorkshire Dales and Morecambe Bay, for example, respectively. Limestone solution has been active, forming the pedestals on which the Norber erratics rest in the Ingleborough area, as well as the many and varied limestone pavements. Erosion has created impressive gorges by the retreat of waterfalls. At Hardrow Scar, for example, in Wensleydale the cyclothem rock strata facilitate this type of erosion, by the undermining of the harder strata in the sequence by erosion of the softer shales.

The greatest change has probably taken place in the post-glacial period around the coasts of Northern England. The rapid rise of sea level in the Flandrian transgression has created entirely new coastline. The changes of sea level have been deciphered by reading the evidence provided by postglacial vegetational changes in relation to features indicating former sea level positions. The evidence is most complete on the Cumbrian and Lancashire coasts. Within the Morecambe Bay coastal zone detailed study of the coastal peats has allowed a chronological sequence of vegetational and sea level changes to be analysed. The coasts of Northumberland and Durham provides a wide variety of coastal scenery, scenery, ranging from cliffs to complex areas of deposition, such as occur in the lee of Holy Island. The Isle of Man also provides many interesting coastal contrasts, from the high cliffs of the hilly southwestern part of the island, to the drift cliffs of the northern part and the storm wave shingle ridges of the extreme northern tip of the island, around the Point of Ayre.

The scenery of Northern England provides a wealth of beauty and interest for the geomorphologist, who can read in the landscape the events that have given rise to its unique qualities. It contains the wild and magnificent scenery of the uplands, in which there is the contrast between the expansive moors of the Pennines, the smooth rounded hills of Cheviot, the Howgills and the southern Lake District, and the rough, knobbly hills of the central Lake District. In between are the gentler stretches of lowland, diversified in places by the following lines of the drumlins. These contrast with the subtler landforms of the Lancashire plain, where the most impressive glacial features are hidden beneath the drift, which fills and buries the ice-ways of Merseyside. The variation in rock types and their resistance to erosion gives rise, in the marginal areas, to the alternation of scarp and dip slopes. Throughout the region there is a close relationship between rock type, structure and scenery.

Bibliography

Papers on the geomorphology of Northern England are fairly widely scattered in the general geological and geographical periodicals. *Field Studies*, the journal of the Field Studies Council, which has a much-used centre at Malham Tarn, also provides material relating to the geomorphology of the area. A number of local and regional journals also carry papers on the geology and geomorphology. These include the *Proceedings of the Yorkshire Geological Society*, the *Scottish Geographical Magazine*, the *Liverpool and Manchester Geological Journal*, now continued as the *Geological Journal*, the *Proceedings of the Isle of Man Natural History and Antiquarian Society*, the *Proceedings of the Cumberland Geological Society*, the *Proceedings of the University of Durham Philosophical Society*, the *Transactions of the Natural History Society of Northumberland and Durham*, and the *Mercian Geologist*.

On the glacial topics material of value can be found in the Quaternary Research Association field guides, while the periglacial processes and features are discussed in papers published in the *Biuletyn Periglacjalny*, and the pollen analysis and vegetational aspects are commented on in the *New Phytologist*. Karst features and cave morphology are discussed in the *Transactions of the Cave Research Group of Great Britain*, and the *Cave Science Journal* of the British Speleological Society. The very useful volume on the *Limestone and Caves of North West England* was published by the British Cave Research Association in 1974.

The literature on Northern England is fairly extensive and covers a wide time span. Some of the early work is still of great value, such as J.G. Goodchild's work on the glaciation of the Eden Valley and Yorkshire Dales, published in 1875. Marr and

Fearnsides (1909) work on the Howgill Fells is still very relevant, and very valuable contributions were made by S.E. Hollingworth and F.M. Trotter on both glaciation and drainage development and morphology in the 1920s and 1930s. The coasts have, on the whole, received less attention, with the exception of R.K. Gresswell's work in Lancashire. Although much work of real value has already been achieved, many aspects of the geomorphology have yet to receive attention.

References

ANDERSON, W. (1939) Possible lateglacial sea-levels at 190 feet and 140 feet in the British Isles. *Geol. Mag.* 76, 317-21.

ANDREWS, J.T. and KING, C.A.M. (1968) Comparative till fabrics and till fabric variability in a till sheet and a drumlin: a small-scale study. *Proc. Yorks. Geol. Soc.* 36, 435-61.

ANDREWS, J.T., KING, C.A.M. and STUIVER, M. (1973) Holocene sea level changes, Cumberland coast, northwest England: eustatic and glacio-isostatic movement. *Geol. en Mijnb.* 52, 1-12.

ANDREWS, J.T. and SMITH, D.I. (1969 (1970)) Statistical analysis of till fabric: methodology, local and regional variability (with particular reference to the north Yorkshire till cliffs.) *Quart. J. Geol. Soc.* 125, 503-42.

ANSON, W.W. and SHARP, J.I. (1960) *Surface and rock-head relief features in the northern part of the Northumberland coalfield.* Univ. of Durham, King's College, Newcastle-upon-Tyne, Dept. of Geogr., Research Series, 2, 23 pp.

ASHMEAD, P. (1969) The origin and development of caves in the Morecambe Bay area. *Trans. Cave Res. Group. G.B.* 11, 201-8.

ASHMEAD, P. (1974) The caves and karst of the Morecambe Bay area. In A.C. Waltham (ed.) *The limestone and caves of northwest England.* Newton Abbot, 201-26.

BEAUMONT, P. (1968) *A history of glacial research in northern England from 1860 to the present day.* Occasional Papers Dept. of Geogr. Durham Univ. 9, 21 pp.

BEAUMONT, P. (1970) *Durham County and City with Teesside.* British Association, J.C. Dewdney (ed.), chap. 2 Geomorphology, 26-45.

BEAUMONT, P. (1971) Stone orientation and stone count data from the lower till sheet, East Durham. *Proc. Yorks. Geol. Soc.* 38, 343-60.

BERRY, W.G. (1967) Salt marsh development in the Ribble Estuary. In R.W. Steel and R. Lawton (eds.), *Liverpool essays in geography* 121-35.

BLACK, W.W. (1958) The structure of the Burnsall-Cracoe district and its bearing on the origin of the Cracoe reef knolls. *Proc. Yorks. Geol. Soc.* 31, 391-414.

DE BOER, G. (1974) Physiographic evolution. In D.H. Rayner and J.E. Hemingway (eds.) *The geology and mineral resources of Yorkshire,* Yorks. Geol. Soc., 271-92.

BOTT, M.H.P. (1964) Gravity measurements in the northeastern part of the Irish Sea. *Quart. J. Geol. Soc.* 120, 369-96.

BOTT, M.H.P. (1967) Geophysical investigations of the northern Pennine basement rocks. *Proc. Yorks. Geol. Soc.* 36, 139-68.

BOTT, M.H.P. (1974) The geological interpretation of a gravity survey of the English Lake District and the Vale of Eden. *J. Geol. Soc. Lond.* 130, 309-31.

BOULTON, G.S. and WORSLEY, P. (1965) Late Weichselian glaciation in the Cheshire-Shropshire basin. *Nature* 207, 704-6.

BOWER, M.M. (1960) Peat erosion in the Pennines. *Adv. of Sci.* 16, 323-31.

BOWER, M.M. (1961) The distribution of erosion in blanket peat bogs in the Pennines. *Trans. Inst. Br. Geogr.* 29, 17-30.

BOWER, M.M. (1962) The cause of erosion in blanket peat bogs: a review of evidence in the light of recent work in the Pennines. *Scot. Geogr. Mag.* 78, 33-43.

BROOK, D. (1971) Caves and caving in Kingsdale. *Cave Sci. J. Br. Spel. Soc.* 6 (48), 33-46.

BROOK, D. (1974) Cave development in Kingsdale. In A.C. Waltham (ed.) *The limestone and caves of northwest England.* Newton Abbot 310-34.

CAINE, T.N. (1963a) The origin of sorted stripes in the Lake District. *Geogr. Ann.* 45, 172-9.

CAINE, T.N. (1963b) Movement of low angle scree slopes in the Lake District, North England. *Rev. Geom. Dynam.* 14, 171-7.

CLAPPERTON, C.M. (1966) The influence of topography on the super-imposition of glacial meltwater streams. *B.R.G.R. Occ. Pap.* 3, 13-18.

CLAPPERTON, C.M. (1968) Channels formed by the superimposition of glacial meltwater streams with special reference to the east Cheviot hills, northeast England. *Geogr. Ann.* 50 A, 207-20.

CLAPPERTON, C.M. (1970a) The evidence for a Cheviot Ice Cap. *Trans. Inst. Br. Geogr.* 50, 115-27.

CLAPPERTON, C.M. (1970b) Channels formed by the superimposition of meltwater streams: a reply to comments by Thorsten Stenborg 1969 Channel formation and glacial drainage. *Geogr. Ann.* 52 (A), 94-5.

CLAPPERTON, C.M. (1971a) The pattern of deglaciation in part of north Northumberland. *Trans. Inst. Br. Geogr.* 53, 67-78.

CLAPPERTON, C.M. (1971b) The location and origin of glacial meltwater phenomena in the east Cheviot Hills. *Proc. Yorks. Geol. Soc.* 38, 361-80.

CLARK, R. (1967) A contribution to glacial studies of the Malham Tarn area. *Field Stud.* 2, 479-91.

CLAYTON, K.M. (1966) The origin of the landforms of the Malham area. *Field Stud.* 2, 359-84.

COLLINSON, J.D. (1970) Deep channels, massive beds and turbidity current genesis in the central Pennine basin. *Proc. Yorks. Geol. Soc.* 37, 495-591.

COMMON, R. (1954) The geomorphology of the east Cheviot area. *Scot. Geogr. Mag.* 70, 124-38.

COMMON, R. (1957) Variation in the Cheviot melt-water channels. *Geogr. Studies* 4, 90-103.

CONWAY, V.M. and MILLAR, A. (1960) The hydrology of some small peat-covered catchments in the northern Pennines. *J. Inst. Water Eng.* 14, 415-24.

COSTER, H.P. and GERRARD, J.A. (1947) A seismic investigation on the outflow of Windermere. *Geogr. Mag.* 84, 224-8

CUBBON, A.M. (1954-6 (1957)) The Ice Age in the Isle of Man. *Proc. Isle of Man Nat. Hist. & Antiq. Soc.* 5, 499-512.

CUMMINS, W.A. (1956) New Quaternary section in Liverpool. *Liverpool and Manchester Geol. J.* 1, 502-6.

DEAN, V. (1947) An unrecorded overflow channel in northeast Lancashire *Proc. Yorks. Geol. Soc.* 27, 33-5.

DEAN, V. (1952) Some unrecorded overflow channels in northeast Lancashire. *Liverpool and Manchester Geol. J.* 1, 153-60.

DERBYSHIRE, E. (1961) Subglacial col gullies and the deglaciation of the north-east Cheviots. *Trans. Inst. Br. Geogr.* 29, 31-46.

DICKSON, C.A. DICKSON, J.H. and MITCHELL, G.F. (1970) The later-Weichselian flora of the Isle of Man. *Phil. Trans. Rov. Soc.* B 258, 31-75.

DINGLE, R.V. (1971) Buried tunnel valleys off the Northumberland coast, western North Sea. *Geol. en Mijnb.* 50, 675-86.

DOUGHTY, P.S. (1968) Joint densities and their relation to lithology in the Great Scar limestone. *Proc. Yorks. Geol. Soc.* 36, 479-512.

DWERRYHOUSE, A.R. (1902) The glaciation of Teesdale, Weardale and the Tyne valley and their tributary valleys. *Quart. J. Geol. Soc.* 58, 572-608.

EASTWOOD, T. et al. (1968) Geology of the country around Cocker-mouth and Caldbeck. 298 pp. *Mem. Geol. Surv.* H.M.S.O.

EVANS, W.B. and ARTHURTON, R.S. (1973) North-west England. In Mitchell et al. *A correlation of Quaternary deposits in the British Isles.* Geol. Soc. London, Special Report 4, 32.

EVANS, W.B., WILSON, A.A., TAYLOR, B.J. and PRICE, D. (1968) The geology of the country around Macclesfield. *Mem. Geol. Surv.* Sheet 110, 182-261 chap. VII. H.M.S.O. 328 pp.

EYRE, J. and ASHMEAD, P. (1967) Lancaster Hole and the Ease Gill Caverns, Casterton Fell, Westmorland, *Trans. Cave Res. Group G.B.* 9, 123 pp.

FALCONER, A. (1972) Use of Q-mode factor analysis in the interpretation of glacier deposits. In E. Yatsu and A. Falconer (eds.), *Research
methods in Pleistocene geomorphology*. Norwich, 148-85

GALLIERS, J.A. (1970) *The geomorphology of Holy Island, Northumberland*. University of Newcastle. Dept. of Geogr. Res. Ser. 6, 34 pp.

GLOVER, R.R. (1974) Cave development in the Gaping Gill system. In
A.C. Waltham (ed.) *The limestone and caves of northwest England*.
Newton Abbot, 343-84

GOLDIE, H. (1973) The limestone pavements of Craven. *Trans. Cave Res.
Group. G.B.* 15, 175-90.

GOODCHILD, J.G. (1875) The glacial phenomena of the Eden valley and
the western part of the Yorkshire Dales district. *Quart. J. Geol. Soc.*
31, 55-99.

GRESSWELL, R.K. (1952) The glacial geomorphology of the southeastern
part of the Lake District. *Liverpool and Manchester Geol. J.* 1, 57-70.

GRESSWELL, R.K. (1953) *Sandy shores in South Lancashire*. Liverpool.

GRESSWELL, R.K. (1956) Note on preglacial lake deposits on the
western side of the Isle of Man. *Liverpool and Manchester Geol. J.* 1,
381-4.

GRESSWELL, R.K. (1958a) The post glacial raised beach in Furness and
Lyth, north Morecambe Bay. *Trans. Inst. Br. Geogr.* 25, 79-103.

GRESSWELL, R.K. (1958b) Hillhouse coastal deposits of south Lancashire. *Liverpool and Manchester Geol. J.* 2, 60-78.

GRESSWELL, R.K. (1962) The glaciology of the Coniston Basin.
Liverpool and Manchester Geol. J. 3, 83-96.

GRESSWELL, R.K. (1964) The origin of the Mersey and Dee estuaries.
Geol. J. 4, 77-86.

GRESSWELL, R.K. and LAWTON, R. (1964) *Merseyside*. British Landscape through maps. 6, Geogr. Assoc. Sheffield.

GRESSWELL, R.K. (1967) The geomorphology of the Fylde In R.W.
Steel and R. Lawton (eds.) *Liverpool essays in geography,* 25-42.

HAY, T. (1944) Mountain form in Lakeland. *Geogr. J.* 103, 263-71.

HEWITT, R.H. (1964) Glacial evidence on the coast between Beckermet
and St Bees. *Proc. Cumb. Geol. Soc.* 2, 25-6.

HIBBERT, F.A., SWITSUR, V.R. and WEST, R.G. (1971) Radiocarbon
dating of Flandrian pollen zones at Red Moss, Lancashire. *Proc. Roy.
Soc. Lond. B* 177, 161-76.

HOLLINGWORTH, S.E. (1929) The evolution of the Eden drainage in the
south and west. *Proc. Geol. Assoc.* 40, 115-38.

HOLLINGWORTH, S.E. (1931) The glaciation of western Edenside and
adjoining areas, and the drumlins of the Edenside and Solway Basin.
Quart. J. Geol. Soc. 87, 281-359.

HOLLINGWORTH, S.E. (1934) Some solifluction phenomena in the northern part of the Lake District. *Proc. Geol. Assoc.* 45, 167-88.

HOLLINGWORTH, S.E. (1936) High level erosional platforms in Cumberland and Furness. *Proc. Yorks. Geol. Soc.* 23, 159-77.

HOWELL, F.T. (1971) A continuous seismic profile survey of Windermere. *Geol. J.* 7, 329-34.

HOWELL, F.T. (1973) The sub-drift surface of the Mersey and Weaver catchment and adjacent areas. *Geol. J.* 8, 285-96.

HUDDART, D. (1967) Deglaciation in the Ennerdale area — a re-interpretation. *Proc. Cumb. Geol. Soc.* 2, 63-75.

HUDDART, D. (1971) Textural distinction of Main Glaciation and Scottish Readvance tills in the Cumberland Lowland. *Geol. Mag.* 108, 317-24.

HUDSON, R.G.S. *et al.* (1933) The geology of the Yorkshire Dales. *Proc. Geol. Assoc.* 44, 227-69.

INGHAM, J.K. (1966) The Ordovician rocks in the Cautley and Dent districts of west Yorkshire. *Proc. Yorks. Geol. Soc.* 35, 455-505.

JOHNSON, G.A.L. (1967) Basement control of Carboniferous sedimentation in northern England. *Proc. Yorks. Geol. Soc.* 36, 175-94.

JOHNSON, G.A.L. (1970) *Durham County and City with Teesside.* British Association. J.C. Dewdney (ed.) chap. 1, Geology, 3-25.

JOHNSON, R.H. (1963) The Roosdyche, Whaley Bridge: a new approach. *East Mid. Geogr.* 3 (19), 155-62.

JOHNSON, R.H. (1965) Glacial geomorphology of the west Pennine slopes. In J.B. Whittow and P.D. Wood (eds.) *Essays in geography for A.A. Miller.* Reading University.

JOHNSON, R.H. (1969) The glacial geomorphology of the area around Hyde, Cheshire. *Proc. Yorks. Geol. Soc.* 37, 189-230.

JOHNSON, R.H. (1969-70) A reconnaissance survey of some river terraces in parts of the Mersey and Weaver catchments. *Mems. and Pres. Manchester Lit. and Phil. Soc.* 112, 35-69.

JOHNSON, R.H. (1971) The last glaciation in northwest England: a general survey. *The Amateur Geol.* 2, 18-37.

JONES, R.J. (1965) Aspects of the biological weathering of limestone pavements. *Proc. Geol. Assoc.* 76, 421-33.

KAY, J.A. (1969) The proposed Solway Firth barrage: a review of the geological and geotechnical aspects. *Eng. Geol.* 3, 265-306.

KENT, P.E. (1966) The structure of the concealed Carboniferous rocks of northeast England. *Proc. York. Geol. Soc.* 35, 323-52.

KENT, P.E. (1974) Structural history. In D.H. Rayner and J.E. Hemingway (eds.) *The geology and mineral resources of Yorkshire.* Yorks. Geol. Soc., 13-28.

KESTNER, F.J.T. (1970) Cyclic changes in Morecambe Bay. *Geogr. J.* 136, 85-97.

KING, C.A.M. (1953) The relationship between wave incidence, wind direction and beach changes at Marsden Bay, Co Durham. *Trans. Inst. Br. Geogr.* 19, 13-23.

KING, C.A.M. (1969) Trend surface analysis of central Pennine erosion surfaces. *Trans. Inst. Br. Geogr.* 47, 47-59.

KING, C.A.M. and ANDREWS, J.T. (1967) Radiocarbon date and significance from the Bride moraine, Isle of Man. *Geol. J.* 5, 305-8.

KING, W.B.R. (1924) River capture in the Lunds, Yorkshire. *Naturalist* 41-4 and 81-3.

KING, W.B.R. (1935) The upper Wensleydale river system. *Proc. Yorks. Geol. Soc.* 23, 10-24.

LEWIS, R.G. (1968) The geology, drainage and speleological prospects of Longliffe, Wharfedale. *Wessex Cave Club Journ.* 10 (120), 200-2.

LEWIS, W.V. (ed.) (1960) *Investigations on Norwegian cirque glaciers.* Roy. Geog. Soc. Res. Ser. 4, 101 pp.

LINTON, D.L. (1957) Radiating valleys in glaciated lands. *Tijdschrift van het Koninklijke Nederland. Aardrijkskundig Genootschap* 74, 297-312.

LINTON, D.L. (1964) Tertiary landscape evolution. In J.W. Watson and J.B. Sissons (eds.) *The British Isles: a systematic geography* 110-30.

LONG, M.H. (1968) Out Sleet Beck Pot, Penyghent, Littondale, Yorks. *J. Br. Speleol. Assos.* 6, (1967), 73-83.

MACKERETH, F.J.H. (1965-6) Some chemical observations on postglacial sediments. *Phil. Trans. Roy. Soc. B.* 250, 165-213.

MAGRAW, D. and RAMSBOTTOM, W.H.C. (1956) A deep borehole for oil at Croxteth Park, near Liverpool. *Liverpool and Manchester Geol. Soc.* 1, 512-35.

MALING, D.H. (1954-7) The shape and nature of the preglacial Wear valley between Cocken and Chester-le-Street. *Proc. Univ. of Durham Phil. Soc.* 12, 14-28.

MANLEY, G. (1959) The lateglacial climate of northwest England. *Liverpool and Manchester Geol. J.* 2, 188-215.

MARR, J.E. (1916) *The geology of the Lake District and the scenery as influenced by geological structure.* Cambridge 232 pp.

MARR, J.E. and FEARNSIDES, W.G. (1909) The Howgill Fells and their topography. *Quart. J. Geol. Soc.* 65, 587-610.

MARSHALL, J.R. (1962) The morphology of the upper Solway salt marshes. *Scot. Geogr. Mag.* 72, 81-99.

MATHER, P.M. (1969) *Analysis of some late Pleistocene sediments from south Lancashire and their relation to glacial and fluvioglacial processes.* Unpubl. Ph.D. thesis, Univ. of Nottingham.

MATTHEWS, B. (1967) Automatic measurement of frost heave: results from Malham and Radley (Yorkshire). *Geoderma* 1, 107-15.

McCONNEL, R.B. (1938) Residual erosion surfaces in mountain ranges. *Proc. Yorks. Geol. Soc.* 24, 76-98.

McCONNEL, R.B. (1939) The relic surfaces of the Howgill Fells. *Proc. Yorks. Geol. Soc.* 24, 152-64.

MELVILLE, W. (1953) Post war protection works at Fleetwood, Lancashire, 1946-1950. *Proc. Inst. Civ. Eng.* 2, 503-9.

MITCHELL, G.F. (1958) A lateglacial deposit near Ballaugh, Isle of Man. *New Phytol.* 57, 256-63.

MITCHELL, G.F. (1965) The Quaternary deposits of the Ballaugh and Kirkmichael districts, Isle of Man. *Quart. Journ. Geol. Soc.* 21, 359-81.

MITCHELL, G.F. (1971) Quaternary Research Association. *Isle of Man Field Guide.* G.S.P. Thomas (ed.) 3-12 mimeo.

MITCHELL, G.F., PENNY, L.F., SHOTTON, F.W. and WEST, R.G. (1973) A correlation of Quaternary deposits in the British Isles. *Geol. Soc.* London, Special Report 4.

MITCHELL, G.H. (1928) The preglacial history of the River Kent, Westmorland. *Proc. Liverpool Geol. Soc.* 15, 78-83.

MITCHELL, G.H. (1931) The geomorphology of the eastern part of the Lake District. *Proc. Liverpool Geol. Soc.* 15, 322-38.

MITCHELL, G.H. (1956) The geological history of the Lake District. *Proc. Yorks. Geol. Soc.* 30, 407-63.

MOISLEY, H.A. (1955) Some karstic features in the Malham Tarn district. *Ann. Rep. Council for the Promotion of Field Studies.* 1953-4, 33-42.

MOSELEY, F. (1961) Erosion surfaces in the Forest of Bowland. *Proc. Yorks. Geol. Soc.* 32, 173-96.

MOSELEY, F. (1972) A tectonic history of northwest England. *J. Geol. Soc. Lond.* 128, 561-98.

MOSELEY, F. (1973) Orientations and origins of joints, faults and folds in the Carboniferous limestone of northwest England. *Trans. Cave. Res. Group. G.B.* 15, 99-106.

MOSELEY, F. and AHMED, S.M. (1967) Carboniferous joints in northern England and their relation to earlier and later structures. *Proc. Yorks. Geol. Soc.* 36, 61-81.

NEAVERSON, E. (1947) Coastal changes around Liverpool Bay since the ice age. *Proc. Liverpool Geol. Soc.* 19, 184-209.

NORMAN, J.W. and WALTHAM, A.C. (1969) The use of air photographs in the study of karst features. *Trans. Cave Res. Group. G.B.* 11, 245-53.

O'CONNOR, J. (1964) The geology of the area around Malham Tarn, Yorkshire. *Field Stud.* 2, 53-82.

OLDFIELD, F. (1960a) Studies in the post glacial history of British vegetation: Lowland Lonsdale. *New Phytol.* 59, 192-217.

OLDFIELD, F. (1960b) Late quaternary changes in climate, vegetation and sea level in lowland Lonsdale. *Trans. Inst. Br. Geogr.* 28, 99-117.

OWEN, D.E. (1947) Pleistocene history of the Wirral peninsula. *Proc. Liverpool Geol. Soc.* 19, 210-39.

OWEN, D.E. (1950) The lower Mersey. *Proc. Liverpool Geol. Soc.* 20, 137-48.

PARRY, J.T. (1960a) The limestone pavements of northeast England. *Canadian Geogr.* 16, 14-21.

PARRY, J.T. (1960b) The erosion surfaces of the southwestern Lake District. *Trans. Inst. Br. Geog.* 28, 39-54.

PENNINGTON, W. (1962) Lateglacial moss records from the English Lake District. Data for the study of postglacial history. *New Phytol.* 61, 28-31.

PENNY, L.F. (1964) A review of the last glaciation in Great Britain. *Proc. Yorks. Geol. Soc.* 34, 387-411.

PEEL, R.F. (1941) The North Tyne valley. *Geogr. J.* 28, 5-19.

PEEL, R.F. (1951) A study of two Northumbrian spillways. *Trans. Inst. Br. Geogr.* 15 (1949) 73-89.

PHILLIPS, A.W. (1968) A seabed drifter investigation in Morecambe Bay. *Dock and Harbour Auth.* 49, 571.

PHILLIPS, A.W. (1969) Sea-bed water movements in Morecambe Bay. *Dock and Harbour Auth.* 49, 580.

PITTY, A.F. (1968) Calcium carbonate content of karst water in relation to through-flow time. *Nature* 217, 939.

PITTY, A.F. (1971) Observations of tufa deposition. *Area* 3, 185-9.

PITTY, A.F. (1972) The contrast between Derbyshire and Yorkshire in the average value of calcium-carbonate in their cave and karst waters. *Trans. Cave Res. Group. G.B.* 14, 151-5.

PITTY, A.F. (1974) Karst water studies in and around Ingleborough Cavern. In A.C. Waltham (ed.) *The limestone and caves of northwest England.* Newton Abbot, 127-39.

PRICE, W.A. and KENDRICK, M.P. (1963) Field and model investigation into the reasons for siltation in the Mersey estuary. *J. Inst. Civ. Engs.* 24, 473-517.

RADLEY, J. (1962) Peat erosion on the high moors of Derbyshire and West Yorkshire. *East. Mid. Geogr.* 3, 40-50.

RAISTRICK, A. (1926) Glaciation of Wensleydale, Swaledale and adjoining parts of the Pennines. *Proc. Yorks. Geol. Soc.* 20, 366-411.

RAISTRICK, A. (1927) Periodicity in the glacial retreat in west Yorkshire. *Proc. Yorks. Geol. Soc.* 21, 24-8.

RAISTRICK, A. (1931) The glaciation of Northumberland and Durham. *Proc. Geol. Assoc.* 42, 281-91.

RAISTRICK, A. (1934) The correlation of glacial retreat stages across the Pennines. *Proc. Yorks. Geol. Soc.* 22, 199-214.

RAMSBOTTOM, W.H.C. (1973) Transgressions and regressions in the Dinantian: a new systhesis of British Dinantian stratigraphy. *Proc. Yorks. Geol. Soc.* 39, 567-607.

RAMSBOTTOM, W.H.C., GOOSSENS, R.F., SMITH, E.G. and CALVER, M.A. (1974) Carboniferous. In D.H. Rayner and J.E. Hemingway (eds.) *The geology and mineral resources of Yorkshire.* Yorks. Geol. Soc., 45-114.

RAYNER, D.H. (ed.) (1974) The geology and mineral resources of Yorkshire. *Yorks. Geol. Soc.* chapter 2, P.E. Kent Structural history 13-28; chapter 9, L.F. Penny Quaternary 245-64; chapter 11, G. de Boer Physiographic evolution 271-92.

ROBSON, D.A. (1966) A guide to the geology of Northumberland and the Borders. *Trans. Nat. Hist. Soc. Northumberland and Durham.* 16, 77 pp.

RODGERS, H.B. (1962) The landscape of east Lancastria. In *Manchester and its region.* Brit. Assoc. 1-16.

ROWELL, A.J. and TURNER, J.S. (1953) Corrie glaciation in the upper Eden valley. *Liverpool and Manchester Geol. Soc.* 1, 200-7.

RYDER, P.F. (1968) Hydrological problems of the west Stainmore area. *Molywarp Spel. Group J.* 2, 25-30.

SHIPP, T. (1962) St Bees and Fleswick beaches. *Proc. Cumb. Geol. Soc.* 1, 21-2.

SHIPP, T. (1964) The Haile-Stockbridge glacial meltwater system. *Proc. Cumb. Geol. Soc.* 2, 10-12.

SHOTTON, F.W. BLUNDELL, D.J. and WILLIAMS, R.E.G. (1970) Birmingham University radiocarbon dates, iv. *Radiocarbon* 12, 385-9.

SIMPSON, E (1967) Malham waters and Pikedaw calamine mine. *J. Br. Spel. Assoc.* 6, 24-9.

SIMPSON, I.M. (1959) The Pleistocene succession in the Stockport and Manchester area. *Quart. J. Geol. Soc.* 115, 107-21.

SIMPSON, I.M. (1960) Stone counts in the Pleistocene of the Manchester area. *Proc. Yorks. Geol. Soc.* 32, 379-88.

SISSONS, J.B. (1958) Subglacial erosion in southern Northumberland. *Scot. Geogr. Mag.* 74, 163-74.

SISSONS, J.B. (1960) Erosion surfaces, cyclic slopes and drainage systems in south Scotland and northern England. *Trans. Inst. Br. Geogr.* 28, 23-38.

SLATER, G. (1931) The structure of the Bride Moraine, Isle of Man. *Proc. Liverpool Geol. Soc.* 15, 284-96.

SMITH, A.G. (1959) The mires of southwestern Westmorland: stratigraphy and pollen analysis. *New Phytol.* 58, 105-27.

SMITH, B. (1912) The glaciation of the Black Coombe district (Cumberland). *Quart. J. Geol. Soc.* 68, 402-48.

SMITH, B. (1932) The glacial lakes of Eskdale, Miterdale and Wasdale, Cumberland and the retreat of the ice during the main glaciation. *Quart. J. Geol. Soc.* 88, 57-83.

SMITH, D.B. and FRANCIS, E.A. (1967) Geology of the country between Durham and West Hartlepool. *Mem. Geol. Surv.* new Ser. sheet 27, H.M.S.O.

SMITH, R.A. (1967) The deglaciation of southwest Cumberland — a reappraisal of some features of the Eskdale and Bootle areas. *Proc. Cumb. Geol. Soc.* 2, 76-83.

SWEETING, M.M. (1950) Erosion cycles and limestone caverns in the Ingleborough district. *Geogr. J.* 115, 63-78.

SWEETING, M.M. (1964) Some factors in the absolute denudation of limestone terrain. *Erdkunde* 18, 92-5.

SWEETING, M.M. (1966) The weathering of limestone, with particular reference to the Carboniferous limestones of northern England. In G.H. Dury (ed.) *Essays in Geomorphology.* 177-210.

SWEETING, M.M. (1974) Karst geomorphology in northwest England. In A.C. Waltham (ed.) *The limestone and caves of northwest England.* Newton Abbot. 46-78.

TAYLOR, B.J. (1958) Cemented shear planes in the Pleistocene Middle Sands of Lancashire and Cheshire. *Proc. Yorks. Geol. Soc.* 31, 359-66.

TEMPLE, P.H. (1965) Some aspects of cirque distribution in the west central Lake District, northern England. *Geogr. Ann.* 47 A, 185-93.

TERNAN, J.L. (1972) Comments on the use of calcium hardness variability index in the study of carbonate aquifers: with reference to the central Pennines, England. *J. Hydrol.* 16, 317-21.

TERNAN, J.L. (1974) Some chemical and physical characteristics of five resurgences on Darnbrook Fell. In A.C. Waltham (ed.) *The limestone and caves of northwest England.* Newton Abbot, 115-26.

THOMPSON, D.B. and WORSLEY, P. (1966) A late Pleistocene molluscan fauna from the drifts of the Cheshire Plain. *Geol. J.* 5, 197-207.

THOMAS, G.S.P. (1971) *Isle of Man Field Guide.* G.S.P. Thomas (ed.) 16-52 Mimeo. Quaternary Research Association.

TOOLEY, M.J. (1974) Sea level changes during the last 9000 years in northwest England. *Geogr. J.* 140, 18-42.

TRECHMAN, C.T. (1931) The 60 ft raised beach at Easington, Co Durham. *Proc. Geol. Assoc.* 42, 295-96.

TRECHMAN, C.T. (1952) On the Pleistocene of east Durham. *Proc. Yorks. Geol. Soc.* 28, 164-79.

TROTTER, F.M. (1929a) The Tertiary uplift and resultant drainage of the Alston block and adjacent areas. *Proc. Yorks. Geol. Soc.* 21, 161-80.

TROTTER, F.M. (1929b) The glaciation of eastern Edenside, the Alston block and the Carlisle plain. *Quart. J. Geol. Soc.* 85, 549-612.

TROTTER, F.M. and HOLLINGWORTH, S.E. (1932) The glacial sequence in the north of England. *Geol. Mag.* 69, 374-80.

TUFNELL, L. (1966) Some little studied British landforms. *Cumb. Geol. Soc. Proc.* 2 (1), 50-6.

TUFNELL, L. (1969) The range of periglacial phenomena in northern England. *Biul. Peryglac.* 19, 291-323.

TUFNELL, L. (1971) Erosion by snow patches in the northern Pennines. *Weather* 26, 492-8.

TUFNELL, L. (1972) Ploughing blocks with special reference to north-west England. *Biul. Peryglac.* 21, 237-70.

WAGER, L.R. (1931) Jointing in the Great Scar Limestone of Craven and its relation to the tectonics of the area. *Quart. J. Geol. Soc.* 88, 392-424.

WALKER, D. (1955a) Skelsmergh Tarn and Kentmere, Westmorland. *New Phytol.* 64, 222-54.

WALKER, D. (1955b) Lateglacial deposits at Lunds, Yorkshire. *New Phytol.* 54, 343-9.

WALKER, D. (1966a) The late Quaternary history of the Cumberland lowland. *Phil. Trans. Roy. Soc. B* 251, 1-210.

WALKER, D. (1966b) The glaciation of the Langdale Fells. *Geol. J.* 5, 208-15.

WALTHAM, A.C. (1970) Cave development in the limestone of the Ingleborough district. *Geog. Journ.* 136, 574-85.

WALTHAM, A.C. (1971) Leck Fell and the Three Counties System. *Cave Sci. J. Br. Spel. Assoc.* 6, 29-32.

WALTHAM, A.C. (1972a) The caves of the Ingleborough district. *Trans. Cave Res. Group. G.B.* 14, 184-5.

WALTHAM, A.C. (1972b) Cavernous depths of Yorkshire. *Geogr. Mag.* 45, 36-43.

WALTHAM, A.C. (ed.) (1974) *The limestone and caves of northwest England.* Newton Abbot (for the British Cave Research Association). 477 pp.

WARD, C. (1970) The Ayres raised beach, Isle of Man. *Geol. J.* 7, 217-20.

WATSON, E. (1971) Remains of pingos in Wales and the Isle of Man. *Geol. J.* 9, 381-92.

WILCOCK, J.D. (1968) New work on the flood pulse technique. *Trans. Cave Res. Group. G.B.* 10, 73-98.

WILLIAMS, P.W. (1968) Suggested technique for morphological analysis of temperate karst landforms. *Br. Geom. Res. Group Occasional Paper* 4, 12-30.

WILSON, J.B. (1967) Palaeoecology studies on shell beds and associated sediments in the Solway Firth. *Scot. J. Geol.* 3, 329-71.

WOOLACOTT, D. (1905) The superficial deposits and pre-glacial valleys of Northumberland and Durham coalfield. *Quart. J. Geol. Soc.* 61, 64-96.

WOOLACOTT, D. (1921) The interglacial problem and the glacial and postglacial sequence in Northumberland and Durham. *Geol. Mag.* 58, 21-32, 60-9.

WOOLACOTT, D. (1922) On the 60-ft raised beach at Easington, Co Durham. *Geol. Mag.* 59, 64-74.

WORSLEY, P. (1967) Problems in naming the Pleistocene deposits of the northeast Cheshire plain. *Mercian Geol.* 2, 51-5.

WORTHINGTON, P.F. (1972) A geotechnical investigation of the drift deposits of northwest Lancashire. *Geol. J.* 8, 1-16.

Appendix

Table 1.1 Correlation Matrices

APPENDIX

Table 1.1 Correlation Matrices

The correlation coefficient for _all_ areas is placed in the matrix to the right of the six correlation coefficients for each of the six districts. Variables V6 and V9 were not correlated for _all_ areas. Note that the matrix is square and symmetric. It is not necessary, therefore, to reproduce the upper right hand half as this is an image of the data in the lower left hand half.

Areas	Area	V1 Abs. Rel.	V2 Rel. Rel.	V3 Sum. Diss.	V4 Vall. Ch.	V5 Mean Slope	V6 Rock Out.	V7 No. of Str.	V8 Dr. Den.	V9 Dr. Patt.	V10 Bifur. Ratio
V1 Absolute Relief	A1	100									
	A2										
	A3										
	A4										
	A5										
	A6										
V2 Relative Relief	A1	00	100								
	A2	02									
	A3	60									
	A4	77									
	A5	90									
	A6	69									
	All	81									
V3 Summit Dissection	A1	31	03	100							
	A2	12	17								
	A3	13	17								
	A4	60	38								
	A5	66	55								
	A6	53	22								
	All	45	63								
V4 Valley Character	A1	37	24	46	100						
	A2	18	08	28							
	A3	58	27	02							
	A4	77	59	43							
	A5	62	50	61							
	A6	53	24	21							
	All	45	35	35							
V5 Mean Slope	A1	03	08	04	38	100					
	A2	08	24	42	03						
	A3	46	44	57	37						
	A4	81	68	42	71						
	A5	89	88	65	42						
	A6	65	75	32	27						
	All	75	91	74	38						

Matrix of values for variables V6–V10 by area (A1–A6). Values are multiplied by 100 and rounded; a bar underneath indicates a negative value.

V6 Rock Outcrops

	C1	C2	C3	C4	C5	C6	C7
A1	34	08		08	34	02	100
A2	34	23		00	07	25	
A3	12	05		48	11	24	
A4	60	37		37	42	57	
A5	0̲8̲	0̲9̲		27	22	2̲3̲	
A6	0̲5̲	0̲7̲		03	14	1̲3̲	

V7 Number of Streams

	C1	C2	C3	C4	C4b	C5	C5b	C6	C6b	C7	C8
A1	64	31	80	25	44	29	26	28	43	14	100
A2	70	02		32		03		09		59	
A3	86	42		06		55		44		12	
A4	62	31		43		64		42		22	
A5	28	35		04		29		15		0̲5̲	
A6	62	12		34		52		18		1̲5̲	

V8 Drainage Density

	C1	C2	C3	C4	C4b	C5	C5b	C6	C6b	C7	C8	C9
A1	29	11	69	06	42	21	22	18	37	09	78	100
A2	54	52		00		01		23		54	65	85
A3	46	20		36		70		11		26	60	
A4	33	21		21		52		17		0̲3̲	81	
A5	27	29		12		17		28		1̲9̲	29	
A6	33	27		11		38		31		1̲2̲	63	

V9 Drainage Pattern

	C1	C2	C4	C5	C6	C7	C8	C9	C10
A1	20	1̲9̲	19	31	40	16	40	4̲6̲	100
A2	27	0̲9̲	18	16	20	0̲1̲	08	02	14
A3	05	0̲4̲	18	25	15	29	10	24	
A4	2̲7̲	0̲7̲	53	17	13	35	49	21	
A5	3̲6̲	4̲0̲	00	41	36	29	1̲6̲	1̲4̲	
A6	05	12	14	11	20	08	1̲9̲	0̲3̲	

V10 Bifurcation Ratio

	C1	C2	C3	C4	C4b	C5	C5b	C6	C6b	C7	C8	C9	C10	C11
A1	30	0̲6̲	32	18	24	0̲1̲	22	02	25	02	32	16	29	100
A2	1̲0̲	1̲0̲		37		03		2̲0̲		2̲0̲	0̲1̲	1̲6̲	08	
A3	07	18		17		40		09		2̲1̲	16	2̲8̲	15	
A4	00	1̲4̲		27		26		20		36	07	2̲3̲	27	
A5	0̲3̲	1̲0̲		01		00		07		1̲4̲	37	3̲5̲	00	
A6	6̲0̲	2̲5̲		56		2̲8̲		13		1̲4̲	73	30	0̲6̲	

A1 Askrigg block
A2 Alston block
A3 Cheviots
A4 Lake District
A5 Solway Lowland
A6 Northumberland coast

Values are multiplied by 100 and rounded, bar underneath indicating negative value.

Subject and Place Index

Ireland, 83
Irish Sea, 6, 19, 31, 59, 84, 86,
    88, 94;
    coast, 158-77
Irt, river, 154, 161
Irthing, river, 36, 37
isostatic adjustment, 14, 151, 152,
    159, 162

joint trends, 6, 63, 72, 74, 75
Jurassic, 26, 30
Jurby Head, 176

karst, 1, 12, 60-81;
    Craven, 66, 69; geomorpho-
    logical controls, 65-7; geological
    controls, 63-5; glaciated, 61, 72;
    Lake District, northeast of, 63;
    Morecambe Bay, 61-3; subter-
    ranean features, 70-82; surface
    features, 67-70; tropical, 61;
    Yorkshire, northwest, 60, 61
karst features,;
    clints, 63, 67-9; dolines, 67;
    76; grikes, 62, 63, 67-70;
    hollows, enclosed, 67, 68;
    hydrology, 65, 70-2; pavements,
    21, 63, 65-7, 69, 70, 72; polje,
    76, pot holes, 5, 64, 68; *Rande-
    bene*, 65; *Rillenkarren*, 69;
    Rinnenkarren, 62; *Rundkarren*,
    62, 69; runnels, 65; shafts, 64,
    72; shakeholes, 67, 72, 76, 77;
    springs, 67; swallow holes, 67;
    tufa, 71; uvalas, 76
Kendal, 21, 63, 118
Kent, valley, 98, 103;
    estuary, 149, 162, 164
Kirkby Lonsdale, 61
Kirkby Stephen, 25, 120
knick point, 41, 53, 54, 97, 148

lake, 30, 102, 123, 132, 144, 145,
    147, 148 *see also* Lake District
    and corrie; ice dammed, 175

Lake District, 3-5, 8, 9, 14, 16-18,
    20, 21, 24-30, 32, 33, 44;
    axis, 32, 33; Backborrow, 103;
    Borrowdale, 123; denudation,
    45-7, 58, 59; Dunmail Raise,
    102; Easedale, 123; Ennerdale,
    123, 134; Eskdale, 123;
    Esthwaite, 145; glaciation, 84-6,
    97-103, 114, 123, 134;
    Haweswater, 97; Kent valley,
    98; Langdale, 99, 102, 123;
    Newby Bridge, 103; periglacial
    features, 136-8, 142, 143; post-
    glacial modification, 143-5;
    Saddleback, 104; Striding Edge,
    102; Troutbeck, 103; Wastdale,
    123; Wastwater, 145; Winder-
    mere, 98, 102, 103, 145
Lamplugh, 19, 139
Lancashire Plain, 22-4, 42, 44, 48,
    49; coast, 161-73; erosion
    surfaces, 48, 49; glaciation,
    93, 94, 96, 97, 109-13; post-
    glacial events, 146-9

Lancaster, 23, 31, 49
law of unequal slopes, 33
Laxey, 58
Leck Beck, 54, 66
Leven valley, 103, 104, 172
Lhen Trench, 133
limestone, 9, 10, 12, 14, 21, 27,
    53, 64, 70, 144
    Coniston, 17; Magnesian, 26,
    116, 117, 152; Main, 15, 50,
    51; Great, 15, 50, 51; Great
    Scar, 12, 54, 61, 65, 67, 71, 72,
    74
Littledale Fell, 10
Littondale, 66, 108
Liverpool, 24, 49, 109, 110, 170,
    171
Lonsdale, Lowland, 149, 150, 161,
    162

Author Index